W9-CEB-761

To my favorite copy editor of 25 years—
beloved wife Becky. As you can see, we
have a unique working style.

Contents

Killer Doubles

Strategies and tactics for better tennis

Rick Altman

Killer Doubles

Strategies and tactics for better tennis
by Rick Altman

September 2014:   First Edition

Published by:
Harvest Books
1423 Harvest Rd.
Pleasanton CA 94566
925.398.6210
www.killerdoubles.net

Copyright © 2014 Rick Altman. All rights reserved. No part of this book may be reproduced or transmitted in any form or by any means, electronic or mechanical, including photocopying, recording, or by an information storage or retrieval system. To seek permission for reprints and excerpts, contact the Publisher above.

Library of Congress Control Number
2014950309

ISBN
978-0-9906331-0-5

Printed in the United States of America

Thanks to...

If it takes a village to write a book on tennis, Northern California is the place to establish the village. This hotbed of tennis houses world-class players, the dynastic Stanford men's and women's teams, a healthy and vibrant USPTA presence, the second-most prominent tennis publication in the world in *Inside Tennis,* and several hundred thousand participants in clubs and leagues all over the area. From this pool, it was not difficult to hand-pick a great team of playing editors.

◆

Marilyn Morrell-Kristal has been around tennis essentially her entire life. A USPTA P1 pro for over 30 years and former tennis director of 18 years, Marilyn played at Texas Christian University and San Jose State before then earning an induction into the Chabot College Hall of Fame. She serves on the Wilson Advisory staff as well as on the USTA Norcal's (deep breath) Tournament committee, Nomiinating committee, Self-Rate Appeals committee, Sportsmanship committee, and the Junior Tennis Council.

None of those activities comes at the expense of playing time, as she plays to her 5.0 rating in USTA senior, adult, and mother-daughter events.

◆

Jon Toney can also count his involvement with the game in the decades. He was a former No. 1-ranked NorCal junior who then went on to play Division 1 tennis at San Diego State and coach Division 1 at UC

Santa Barbara. He was the head pro at Diablo Country Club for over 10 years, and remains active as a private instructor and formidable 4.5 senior.

His favorite claim to fame: wins over an Evert and an Austin. That would be brothers Drew Evert and Doug Austin…

♦

Which brings me to **Dan Marx**, my lifelong friend of nearly 40 years. He has observed my love affair with the game of tennis from afar and once in a while from near, having made fun of me from the stands on more than one occasion.

Fast forward several decades, and it is now he, in his 50s, who has fallen in love with the game. He zealously plays four times a week, and as an aspirant to 3.5 levels and beyond, was a perfect candidate to provide his feedback. He claims that he no longer hugs his alley when his partner serves.

♦

Finally, a tremendous shout-out to two generous photographers: **Mike Lawrence** is the talent whose work graces our cover, with permission from the USTA. An assistant photo editor for Time Inc., Mike started out with *Racquetball Magazine* with a manual focus 35mm film camera. You can see more of his great work at www.mikelawrencephoto.com.

Kristen Morse, who took the back cover photo of yours truly, is seeing her star rise at Boston College. As Yearbook editor for her high school and team photographer for the softball team on which she and my daughter Jamie played (and I coached), her budding photo and video skills were obvious at an early age.

Foreword

One of the best things about tennis is its variety. It is played on asphalt, concrete, grass, carpet, and dirt. It is played indoors and outdoors, and in just about every country in the world. The ATP has over 70 tournaments in 30 countries and on six continents. We are fortunate to have visited practically every one, and we're happy to see that, anywhere we go, on a Saturday morning at a local club or park, 80% of the play will be doubles.

We love doubles and have enjoyed playing together since we were five years old. We have always had a blast with the team thing: two guys out there working together, pumping each other up when the other is down, enthusiastic congratulations on great shots, high fives...and yes, even chest bumps! Walking on and off court together. Celebrating a win together. Consoling each other after a loss.

Watch a doubles match and you will always see more smiles than in a singles match. Way more smiles. You'll see more laughs, too. Way more. Singles is checkers and doubles is chess. The best doubles points are lightning quick, complex, and more spectacular than the best singles points.

Wonder where serve-and-volley players are today? Go watch a doubles match. Serving and volleying is alive and well there. And with doubles you'll see two people from the same city playing together, or maybe from the same school. Friends playing together. You might see a Democrat playing with a Republican. A doctor with a lawyer. A mom and her son. A dad and his daughter. A husband and wife. A grandpa and a grandson. Players from different parts of the world playing together. Two players of different and perhaps contentious religions playing together—yes, doubles can be a unifying force for world peace. Why should juniors and adults play doubles? Let us count the ways:

- It's fun and social.

- It gives them a second chance in tournaments.

- It will round out their skills.

- It teaches additional life lessons.

- It's a way of getting four people on a court rather than just two at a club whose courts are in short supply.

- It broadens the overall appeal of the sport.

- There are lots of thrills, chills, and adventure as our friend Billie Jean King would like to say. (By the way, Billie Jean's favorite part of a Davis Cup tie is the Saturday doubles and we have always appreciated her being there to root us on in our matches.)

- We are one of the few sports that have men and women competing together—we need to cherish that. You can talk about gender equity all day, or you can just go watch or play a mixed doubles match.

◆

As we read this book on doubles, we found ourselves nodding our heads in agreement. You will enjoy the read and find it loaded with concepts that will help you improve your game. We even learned a few new things and can't wait to try them out.

As this book goes to press, we have just won our 100th title at the U.S. Open, our 16th Grand Slam doubles title, and our 22nd Davis Cup match. We say thanks to you for your support through the years and thanks for your support of the great game of doubles.

After reading this book, we are betting that you will win your next doubles match on Saturday morning. And we know for sure that you will have a smile on your face the whole time. Thanks to Rick for writing this great new book on doubles.

Mike and Bob Bryan

Introduction

The server arches his back and sends a heavy twist into the corner of the ad court, knowing that it will spell trouble for the receiver's one-handed backhand. The receiver knows better than to try to be aggressive with this high-kicking serve, and besides, the server's partner is left-handed, so a low, quick lob return will travel over his backhand. The server can't get there in time to hit an overhead and knows that a sharp cross-court volley would leave too much court exposed, so he plays a safe but firm volley down the line, back to the receiver's backhand. But the receiver's partner has reviewed all of this, not in his head so much as with his instincts, and is already two steps past the center line. His knifed backhand volley splits the court for a well-deserved point against serve.

How often do your points feature this much finesse and acumen? Maybe only one out of 20, but the mere prospect of the delicious chess match that is competitive doubles is enough to keep us returning to the court, day after day, season after season, decade after decade.

If you seek a book that explores strokes and physical fundamentals, this is not the one for you. You'll be able to count on one hand the instances in which I discuss stroke mechanics. But if you seek a deeper appreciation of doubles strategy, if you want to better understand the dynamics of competitive doubles, if you want to inch closer to mastery of the nuance of this wonderful game, and if you want a book that you can actually enjoy, not just study, go ahead and click that Buy Now button.

This book places in its crosshairs adult players like you and me who play in USTA leagues and in local club events. We do not aspire to play open tournaments or earn a national ranking. We play in men's and women's leagues whose NTRP numbers start with a 3 or a 4, mixed and combo leagues of all designations, and intermediate and advanced mixers everywhere. Our best tennis might or might not still be ahead of us, but we know our ceilings. We are amateurs who sit in awe of the Top 4 in the men's game and the parade of European women who hit with more authority than we could ever imagine.

Unlike most authors of tennis books, I did not play at Wimbledon and I received no scholarship offers to play in college. Nobody has ever asked me for my autograph and no company pays me to wear its stuff or even gives me free stuff. And that's what qualifies me to be at my keyboard right now: I know the game that you play. I've been playing it for my entire adult life. I have played alongside 3.5 men and women and I have been on the court against 6.0 guys.

I could throw a few credentials your way, like a pair of national championships in 10.0 mixed and an undefeated season at the 5.5 level. But that was a lifetime ago, before rampant inflation compelled the USTA to devalue its currency, and practically overnight, turn me into a 5.0 player. The passage of time has presided over the rest of my descent, down to my place on 4.5 rosters today. I win more than I lose, but I don't dominate. I struggle with wild fluctuations in focus, energy, and confidence, just like most aging tennis players.

Through these pages, I won't preach at you and I won't ask you to remember a litany of unfamiliar phrases. I won't expect you to take notes and I won't give you homework assignments for the next time you play. And you do not need to read this book from start to finish—you can browse it and flip through it, stopping at any passage that sounds interesting.

These chapters are uneven—some of them a few pages and others a few dozen—and that reflects the coverage of topics, where biases are obvious, not hidden. And not just mine: when any one of my playing editors has a contrary point of view, I do more than just take it into consideration; I invite him or her to share it with you. Disagreement is good, don't you agree?

Similarly, I neither expect nor hope that you will agree with all of my assertions; in fact, if you do, your experience might be a bit diminished.

Tennis is too mysterious and there are too many legitimate and disparate points of view about effective doubles play for us to believe that we can have consensus. And besides, the greatest reward of all might be in the debate and I invite you to partake in it at the Killer Doubles Facebook page.

If I did my job across these 147 pages, this book holds equal appeal across lines of gender and aptitude. While the sweet spot is the 3.5, 4.0, and 4.5 camps, it's not like these concepts are lost on 3.0 players, nor is it inconceivable that 5.0s and 5.5s can't be reminded of things they take for granted.

I have played as much, if not more, mixed doubles than men's doubles. I have all girls in my household. I have two sisters. My mother was the stronger personality in the house while growing up. Even our dog is a girl. I know the women's game practically as well as I know my own game. But, news flash, I'm not actually a woman. If you think there is a female point of view that I am completely missing, write to me at rick@killerdoubles.net, and I'll make sure it is represented in our next edition, which, thanks to the miracle of self-publishing, might be sooner than you think.

On that note, I have made every effort to be even-handed in the often-grammatically-suspect pursuit of proper use of pronouns. I alternate between him and her when it doesn't matter, try to point out the times when it does matter, and stop short of making you dizzy with a bunch of "his or her" constructions. Let me know how I did on that score, too.

◆

So let's get started. Just about every point of view that I will share, each stratagem or tactic offered, all of the philosophy espoused can be traced back to three axioms that I have developed in my 40 years of playing competitively:

1. Good doubles teams win by controlling the middle of the court.

2. When in doubt, hit the ball crosscourt.

3. Confidence does not come from a belief that you can hit any shot, but from knowing which shots you really can hit.

If you already place into practice those three principles, you can stop reading right now. If you would like to explore these axioms with more depth, this is the right read for you.

Doubles Fundamentals

Don't let the name of this first part fool you—you'll get no "bend your knees and watch the ball" stuff from me. Even though I was a USPTA-certified teaching pro back in the day, there are plenty of folks more qualified than I to teach strokes. However, doubles strategy has a set of fundamentals, also, and for the league player, for the doubles enthusiast, for the weekend warrior whose strokes and mechanics became permanent fixtures long ago, these fundamentals will prove more valuable.

Much of these three short chapters have to do with whose role it is to maintain a rally and whose role it is to end a point. Yes, winning in doubles often comes down to knowing when *not* to go for winners.

1

Paying Homage To Crosscourt

Strokes will come and go, grips fall in and out of fashion, and oncourt strategies ebb and flow. But few concepts maintain their enduring value like the crosscourt. Hitting crosscourt is the ultimate chicken soup of tennis: it will rarely hurt you. The first time I remember hearing this concept discussed was by Vic Braden, the tennis guru of the 1970s. He was giving a televised clinic (which means it must have been raining at a tournament somewhere, because back then, he was the go-to filler for rain delays) and he cited the following statistics: The person who changes the direction of a rally has a 75% chance of losing the point. "If you are in a crosscourt rally," he preached, "keep hitting it crosscourt. The person who gets impatient first and hits down the line usually loses!"

His advice was in reference to singles competition, where the strategies are more blunt. A capable doubles team will prevail if you become too predictable, but the principle is still sound. I would state it this way: If you are unable to end a point with your next shot, return it crosscourt. If you can't hit a winner, work hard to set up your partner to be able to hit one. The best way to do that is with a penetrating crosscourt stroke.

The figure below shows this in its most basic form with the server and returner sparring. Whether they hit groundstrokes, volleys, or half-volleys is not really relevant; in all cases, the ball would get pushed deep and crosscourt if a winner cannot be struck. This is the basic meter of doubles:

- Players further from the net should hit crosscourt

- Crosscourt shots should be hit deep

This is like the appetizer for the book—it is a tactic that you have probably been employing for most of your playing career without conscious awareness of it. Hitting crosscourt helps you avoid the danger of the net person, it affords the safest stroke (net lower in the middle), and it provides the longest distance in which a shot can be hit into the court. From this simple formula flows practically the entire tapestry of doubles.

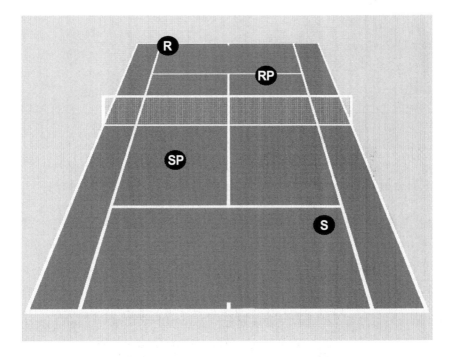

As basic as it gets

Server (S) and returner (R) want to get themselves or their partners (SP and RP) into a position to hit a winner. If that is not possible, their best move is to engage in a crosscourt rally.

2

The Closer

If the crosscourt hitter is the one who starts and sustains points, the person closer to the net is the one who is best positioned to finish them. This is typically the server's partner, and we dedicate an entire chapter to his or her responsibilities and opportunities to end points. It can also be the receiver's partner, who is not ignored in Chapter 7.

As the closer, your job is essentially the opposite of that of the crosscourt player: you seek to end points, not sustain them. You do it by hitting directly at someone, not back to the crosscourt player. And you look to hit short, not long. Look at the diagram on the facing page—if you are the server's or the receiver's partner, you start the point closer to the net than either one of them, and if you are able to get your racquet on a ball, you will want to hit short (at the tops of shoelaces), not deep.

Closers are typically more dangerous when they can move toward the middle with forehand volleys and that is one of the delightful games within the game that better players employ. On offense, they will seek every opportunity to get those forehands in the middle, including playing I-formation (discussed in Chapter 15) and planning crosses that are not necessarily poaches. Meanwhile, smart defenders will lob just to force players to switch sides away from their net strengths.

The promised land here? A lefty-righty combination in which both players have their forehands in the middle. I know that I am going to have to devote pages somewhere to tactics for playing against left-handers, but I'm conflicted. There's a limit to how many secrets I'm willing to give away. Maybe I'll have one of my playing editors write that section…

◆

A point that we take for granted through these concepts is that most doubles is played in a staggered formation. I do not refer to one-up / one-back positioning, which will be the subject of the next chapter, but rather a natural fluidity in which one person is inevitably nearer to the net than the other. The closer always is looking forward while the back player covers the lobs, looks for short balls, and above all, is ready to push the ball back deep and crosscourt.

Aggressive teams will hug the net more and quicker players will cheat in as close as the closer, but they know that they are still responsible for covering lobs and will still default to hitting crosscourt.

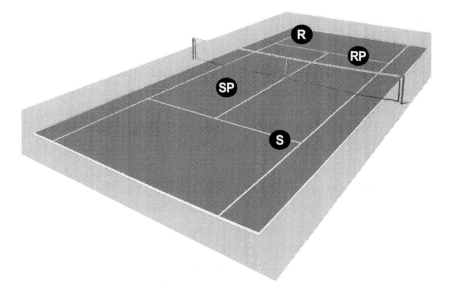

Closing = Winning

The players closest to the net are the ones most apt to end points, and if they get the opportunity, they hit their volleys short (directly at the closest opponent), not long into the court.

3

One Up and One Back

You know that racquet technology has gotten out of hand when tour-level doubles teams choose to play groundstrokes over volleys. First it was the serve-and-volley game that was overwhelmed by the power in today's game, and now it is the very foundation of doubles being threatened.

Fortunately, that is not the case at our level, and I remain strident that the best amateur doubles teams feature partnerships looking to seize control of the net.

That said, playing one up and one back is commonplace and completely viable in almost all levels of the game. While any baseline specialist might prefer staying back, it holds especially true for women. In my 8.0 and 9.0 mixed matches (most mixed leagues identify levels based on the combined ranking of the partnership), practically all of my partners hit groundstrokes until drawn in, and as I think back to the seasons in which our 10.0 mixed doubles teams were competing against the best teams in the country, more than half of my partners served and stayed back and almost all of them returned and stayed back. Ditto for our female opponents.

Please indulge the generalization: women players are just so incredibly steady. When I drill with strong women, I would get eaten for lunch if I did not allow myself to look for balls to approach on. And one of my favorite situations in mixed doubles is the times, however infrequent, in which our male opponent finds himself in a baseline rally with my partner. I almost feel sympathy for him.

When you are engaged in a baseline rally with another woman, in women's or mixed doubles, the criterion is very simple: can you win the rally? Are you a better baseliner than your opponent? If you can answer yes, your course is clear: you bleed your opponent to death. Rally until the sun goes down. Frustration and impatience will often follow, your opponent will start attempting winners or inadvisable pass attempts down the line. Even if she lands a few of them, that's when you know you've got her.

You will likely have to stave off challenges from a strong net player in this scenario, particularly in mixed, and even more particularly if you are rallying deuce court to deuce court and facing a right-handed man with his forehand volley in the middle. You might have to keep him honest with lobs or pass attempts, but don't overreact. Don't freak out if he picks off one or two. Don't change tactics until he becomes a legitimate threat to your holding serve. We'll devote more discussion to the wisdom (or folly) of changing tactics in Chapter 8.

But what if you can't answer yes? What if the woman you face is steadier or more forceful than you? Now it is your side that must change the course of the game and risk becoming the ones who play with frustration or impatience. Lobbing over the net person will only get you so far, as you are likely to find yourself still stuck in a rally with her—now a down-the-line rally, which will favor the stronger player even more. And can you really turn the pass attempt down the alley into a winning strategy? That's the tennis equivalent of drawing to an inside straight; the odds are just not with you.

I'm not suggesting you abandon all efforts to hit lobs and passes. You might discover that the woman covering the lob doesn't move laterally as well as she strokes. And down-the-line attempts do not have to be winners to be effective. You might find a net player whose reflex volleys are not what they used to be, and so instead of going for winners, you can choose the more forgiving target of hitting right at the net person.

All of this is part of the arsenal to defend against being out-rallied, but by far the best defense against the player who will beat you from the baseline is to move one or both of you off the baseline. Rare is the steady player who is equally comfortable at the net, and the low, short, sharp-angled

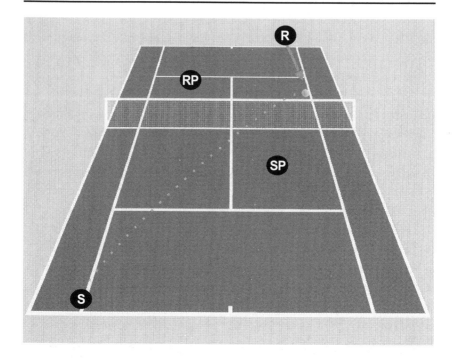

Short balls can kill

If you are being outrallied by a steady baseliner, just about any short ball that draws her to the net might produce a better result.

stroke can be quite the equalizer. And in many cases, the attempt doesn't even have to be that good; a bad drop shot that lands near the service line and sits up will still serve to draw her in.

But I've got a better idea still. Don't be that player who is uncomfortable moving forward. Be the player who relishes an advance on the net, or at least has approached the net so many times in practice matches to have reached a degree of comfort. If you believe that you are more comfortable at the net than she is, you will have completely neutralized her advantage. Even if it is not true. Let me restate that and refer you to Chapter 23 where I recommend fooling yourself: even if there is no evidence to support the claim, if you make yourself believe that you can beat her in a net exchange, you can make it come true.

Improving your confidence at the net is the very best defense against the player who can out-rally you from the baseline. So how do you make that happen? It's too trite to answer "with lots of practice," but how you practice is key. Most of us practice by playing practice sets and matches, and I hold no illusion that you will decide instead to go out and actively engage in a series of net-rushing drills. Your court time is precious, I know, and you want to play sets and matches. Therefore, you must impose your own set of rules on your practice sets. "Tonight, for these next two practice sets, I will follow every other serve to the net, approach on every short ball, and never stay at the service line (or worse, back off of it) when I am the receiver's partner."

Don't try to comfort yourself with the belief that practice matches don't count. You want them to count. You want there to be stakes associated with this. You want to try to win with these tactics, not just see how it feels. And if you lose, you want it to hurt. That is how you become more comfortable with a new tactic—by exposing it to pressure.

And in one of those rare times when I will write about form and technique, this change in tactic might necessitate a change in grip. Most baseliners who have trouble transitioning to the net do so because they can't let go of their beloved western grip on the forehand or two-handed grip on the backhand. But you must. In order to become an accomplished forehand volleyer, you must move your first knuckle to the top, practice tucking in your elbow, and learn to knife your forehand volleys with underspin. Hitting backhand volleys with two hands is not impossible, but the same challenge exists: you must stop swinging and start punching.

And for a change this fundamental, you do need to start away from match conditions. You need to hit hundreds of balls with a new technique to develop sufficient muscle memory. Then you can take these new grips and techniques out for a test drive over practice sets. And when you do, resist the temptation to revert back at 4-5 30-30. Let me chart this out for you: on the continuum of benefits. With zero benefit being on the far left and maximum benefit being on the far right, here is where I would place the three possible outcomes:

Switching back to your old habits		Staying with your new game and losing	Staying with your new game and winning
Zero benefit			**Max benefit**

You'll know you have made great strides when you feel ready to implement your new move in a real match. And when that time comes, I hope you have the courage of conviction and determination to see it through, no matter the outcome. Many sports legends have said it and I'm certain that I will quote them more than once across these pages: learning how to win has a lot to do with how you handle losing.

Beyond the Fundamentals

I was so sure that it was the right move. He had crowded the net all day and my swift and stealthy lob promised to leave him flat-footed and cause his partner to sprint back to retrieve it. We would then take the net and seize control of this break point.

None of that happened. My net-crowding opponent had taken two big steps back before I had even made contact with the ball. It was as if he was in my head. How did he do that? How had he developed such well-honed instincts for the game?

This seminal moment took place about 35 years ago, after which I vowed to become like him. Did it work? Well, 15 years later I got a rematch against him and he beat me again. But much of what I have learned over the years can find its roots in that one match three decades ago in which I was not just beaten, but mastered. Have I said recently about how much more you learn from losing than from winning?

4

Two Choices
Instead of Three

I've been a net rusher my entire life. In my singles-playing days, it was not uncommon for me to play matches in which I would approach the net on every single first serve, nearly every second serve, and on a majority of second-serve return points. I miss the days when racquets were less powerful and angles, quickness, and guile were even more valuable commodities than they are today.

I remember in the early 1980s when John McEnroe figured out how to get the edge on Ivan Lendl, after Lendl won several of their matches in a row, including the French and U.S. Open finals. McEnroe had become too passive and had conceded too much credit to Lendl's powerful groundstrokes. He had even ceded the net to Lendl, allowing Ivan's net advancements to result in easy volley winners.

I sat courtside at the old Cow Palace near San Francisco when McEnroe and Lendl faced off in the finals of the Transamerica Open. McEnroe had clearly thought about things and concluded that, not only could he not allow Lendl to get cheap points at the net, he couldn't allow himself to get stuck in long rallies. He was perhaps the best volleyer in the game and he needed to leverage that.

So he began advancing on every opportunity. Any time he could get a ball to Lendl's backhand, he followed it to the net. Many of the approaches weren't very good, just kind of dumped into the court, but he then turned things over to his hands, his feet, and those sensational volleying instincts.

That summer was the genesis of a two-year run of victories that McEnroe would enjoy over Lendl and I was fortunate enough to be able to have an extended question-and-answer session with him about it. (Normally in press conferences, you are lucky to be able to ask one question and get one follow-up.)

Me: This was a different McEnroe-Lendl match. You intentionally hit to his backhand and took the net as often as you could.

McEnroe: In our last couple of matches, he was dictating the points and moving me around the baseline too much. I just realized that I had to play quicker points and get to the net more.

Me: His backhand is steadier than his forehand, and yet you hit just about every approach to his backhand.

McEnroe: When I could get the ball deep to his backhand, I noticed that he was not able to hit that angled crosscourt, so I could get in position to hit backhand volleys.

Me: But some of your approaches were not deep. They were short and they even sat up.

McEnroe: I know, but on those he was not able to lob, so I figure that I still had an advantage.

That night, I spent the entire 45-minute drive home utterly consumed by McEnroe's analysis. As a fellow left-handed net rusher, he served as my role model for strategy and playing style. Born one month apart and of similar physique, he represented a more skilled version of me. From those incredible press seats at the Cow Palace (on the floor, barely 10 feet behind the baseline, separated by a row of potted plants), I would study his corkscrew service motion, his use of court geometry, and how he would apply and remove pace from the ball. In all areas except for oncourt behavior, I aspired to be like John McEnroe.

Also, he was honest and candid. In fact, he was honest to a fault—that's what got him into so much trouble. But you would always get a straight answer from him, even about strategy that many players on the tour would never reveal.

Can you take away one option?

From watching McEnroe play Lendl, I learned an invaluable point of strategy that I used for nearly two decades of subsequent singles play. Today, almost 35 years later, I still employ those same tactics in doubles matches.

In a basic battle against a person at the net, the defender has three potential options: pass down the line, pass crosscourt, or lob. McEnroe was such a good volleyer that the only time the person at the baseline had the upper hand was if all three of those options were available. If he could take any one of them away, the advantage swung in his favor. And if he could put an opponent in a position in which he had only one option, it was all over.

We don't volley as well as McEnroe but that's okay—our opponents don't defend as well as Lendl did. The same principles apply at our level: if you can reduce an opponent's choices to two, you can take control of the net and the point. Doubles is more nuanced than singles and so this plays out in ways that are a bit more subtle. Nonetheless, you can begin to recognize the patterns.

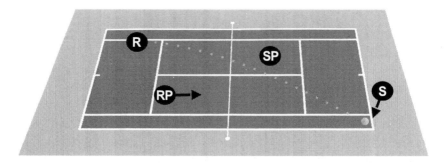

If you (R) get a second serve in the ad court and the server (S) elects to stay back, a deep return into his or her alley will eliminate the crosscourt option for all but the best ball strikers and increase the probability of a lob. Your partner should camp on the net and you should prepare to hit an overhead. (Arrows indicate relevant movement by players.)

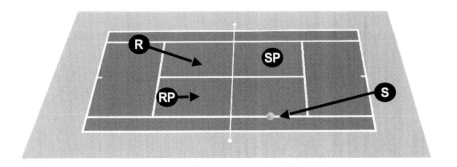

If you dump a ball short, causing your opponent to dash forward, you have virtually eliminated the lob as a possible response. Close tightly and try to volley down.

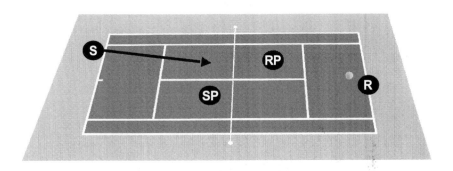

If you serve and hit your first volley deep and down the middle, you have effectively eliminated both angles. You should cover the middle of the court, ready for a drive or a lob.

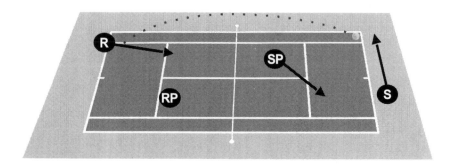

If you lob over an opponent's alley, there is an excellent chance that the response will be a lob back or a drive down the line.

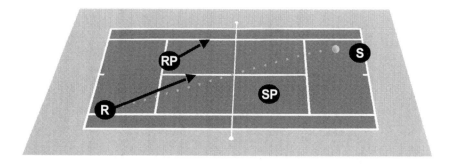

If you bust a ball at an opponent's forehand in the deuce court, it is unlikely that he will have time to return with a sharp crosscourt.

In all of these cases, you have a potential advantage because you have taken away one of your opponents' three options. Good volleyers will only be at disadvantages when all three options are in play.

There is a fourth option for the defense, and it often stands as the best one if your opponents at the net have taken away one of your other three. The fourth option is to hit the ball right at the volleyer. At a minimum, this buys you another swing, and in a way, it takes away one of *their* options, as they will likely not be able to angle off a volley from that position. You have bought yourself a stalemate, from which you might be able to push them off the net, join them at the net, or force an error.

In my prime, I did not consider this to be a viable option, because I believed that any ball hit right at me, no matter how hard, was an opportunity for me to hit a volley winner. Being older and wiser doesn't serve me well because I know better, but there was a time when blissful ignorance was a powerful weapon against reality. Once again, see Chapter 23 in which I extol the virtues of lying to yourself.

5

Identifying Weapons

Implicit in the discussion of limiting opponents' options is the question of which option you limit. It's hardly rocket science to suggest that you want to take away the option that your opponent would prefer to have. Would that it be that simple; if it were, you could get an exhaustive scouting report from your captain and be off to the races.

There are several reasons why being that well informed might not be a good idea, but let's start the conversation at its more vital point: do you know what your own weapons are?

I would suspect that every single person reading this chapter has an answer to that question. I want you to go deeper, however, because too many less-experienced players do not properly think through how their weapon becomes an advantage. A lot of advanced players neglect this, too.

Let's say that you have identified your best weapon as your first serve. You hit it big and you rack up a lot of service winners. And if that scenario doesn't ring true for you, switch it to your two-handed backhand, which you drive deep from the ad side and force errors from surprised opponents. Or a backhand volley that you knife like butter.

All fine and well. Do you have a game plan for when the ball is returned? If not, you do not have a weapon, you have a liability, and if I only had a nickel for the number of times I have said to a partner or a teammate: "His serve is big, but if you just get it back, he'll get flustered and probably dump a volley." In order to truly identify and cultivate your weapon, you need to complete the following sentence:

My serve is a weapon because when I hit it deep into the corner, it usually produces a _____, which allows us to then hit a _____.

It's just not that common for players to go an entire match and not figure out how to deal with one of your shots, no matter how strong it is. The true potential of a weapon is in the way it allows you to craft a point.

This is an easy concept for me to understand because I am not a hard hitter and so my weapons rarely produce winners all by themselves. Therefore, I play this game all the time:

My weapon is a serve that I can always direct to the backhand, enabling me to hit a backhand crosscourt volley when I am in the ad court and setting up a punch volley right down the middle when I am in the deuce court.

My weapon is my quickness, which allows me to get to the net sooner than most, enabling me to take time away from my opponents and hit down on more volleys, producing weak responses.

My weapon is a chip return that lands at the feet of oncoming volleyers, forcing them to hit up, which in turn allows my partner to seize the middle of the court, close on the net, and hit a volley from a forceful position.

One of the qualities that these three sentences share is that they are not constructed very well, grammatically speaking. In fact, I had to veto the edits suggested by my copy editor. They are intended to be run-on sentences; that's what makes them helpful. You want to string together as many causes and effects as you can. That's what forces you to think beyond the single stroke that you initially identified as a weapon. More likely for us amateurs, a true weapon is a series of strokes.

Now let's shift the focus back to the opponents, because it is this very thought process that helps you identify their strengths and weaknesses. First off, I want to suggest that it is not always helpful to have an entire scouting report on your opponents delivered to you by your captain or teammate, however well-intended the effort. I have more to say about this in Chapter 19, but suffice it to say for now that you never want advice received by others to short-circuit your own investigation and discovery. Information you glean about an opponent from the early stages of a match will always be more helpful than a scouting report based on past events. Start with conventional wisdom and go from there:

- Usually players' forehands are better than their backhands. Is that true for our opponents today?

- I normally like to serve middle and that will feed into his gigantic forehand. What does that mean for how we approach points in the ad court?

- He is 6' 4" and during warm-up, his overhead looked like a dream. Should we avoid the lob altogether or first determine if he moves back well?

- In mixed doubles, we usually want to hit most shots to the woman. Is that the case today? Is she really weaker than her male partner?

Thinking critically through a match is a learned skill, but more important, it is not a skill you need learn or practice by yourself. There is no better purpose for talk between partners than ferreting out playing characteristics and discussing patterns and tendencies. You and your partner each warmed up with a different opponent and you can start there. Did he slice his backhand or come over it with two hands? Did she turn her shoulders while at the net or tend to hit "frying pan" volleys? Did he hit mostly flat serves or hit with spin and depth?

You can't draw too many conclusions from warmup, lest I require you to read Chapter 18, Psych Up or Psych Out? It's vital to keep collecting intelligence as the match ensues, and to that end, you are looking for particular strokes that opponents miss, hit weakly, or more likely, actively avoid. Then you must ask yourself how you can match up your own strengths with those areas of weakness.

It happened on court

Case in point: a women's 4.0 match I watched recently. One of the opponents of the home team, a gal named Ginny, hit great waist-level volleys and was confident with half-volleys. However, when provided with a floater, she would often overreact, rush with her upper body, root her feet, and mishit the volley. This is not at all uncommon among us weekend hackers—we make the hard shots and miss the easy ones!

On the other side, Team Carla (I didn't get her partner's name) noted that Ginny missed two high forehand volleys in a row. "Let's keep feeding those to her," Carla said.

This strategy saw Team Carla lose the first set 6-2 in about 15 minutes. Ginny hit putaway after putaway and Team Carla wandered around in a daze. "She must have hit 10 of those in a row," Carla said later.

What mistake did Team Carla make? They correctly identified the weakness but misdiagnosed the course of action. In hitting soft balls to Ginny, they disregarded the strengths of their own game, and by intentionally hitting floaters to Ginny, they essentially served up batting practice to her. Ginny didn't miss those high forehands because she was necessarily bad at them; anyone can hit those shots when ready for them. She initially mishit them because she overreacted when expecting a more aggressive play.

Team Carla's captain realized this and intervened. "Offering up sitters is not your game," she said. "You two have really good hands at the net so get up there and volley. But don't worry about hitting winners, just get balls back. If you reflex a ball to Ginny, that's when she might overhit. If you get a ball you can hit a winner off of, great. But if not, just keep making her hit forehand volleys. Sooner or later the difference in pace will throw her off."

This plan worked perfectly. Ginny's real weakness was in determining the pace of oncoming shots and reacting properly. With waist-high volleys, there is not much reaction required, but on high volleys, a more complicated series of mechanics is put in place (racquet back, head up, move forward, hit slightly down). With volley exchanges of varied pace, Ginny lost her ability to time her strokes and then lost her confidence.

Team Carla effectively matched up their own strengths with the weakness of their opponent. They won in a super tiebreaker.

6

The Value of the Slice Backhand

A majority of the women I play against hit with two hands on their backhand side. Depending upon the age group, anywhere from 25% to 50% of the men do, as well. This means I have to brace myself for a lot of hard-hit and penetrating returns and groundstrokes, most likely with quite a bit of topspin. It also means that I won't see many returns hit with slice, and I'll take the trade.

The slice backhand has become the orphan of modern-day tennis. You rarely see it on television and the preponderance of two-handers in our local ranks has helped make it part of a dying breed.

I'm not going to go all Luddite on you or bemoan the death of the good old days. Further, if you can hit a penetrating topspin backhand under pressure, you'd be wise to keep doing it. Here, however, are a few of the reasons why you should consider hitting the slice more often, or incorporate it into your game if you don't already own a slice backhand.

It's the safer shot

Most players who own a slice backhand would acknowledge that it can be hit in the court with a higher percentage, when compared with a topspin backhand. That simple fact should not be ignored or downplayed, given that most points end in error. Check out this 2011 Tennis Channel report on the percentage of points that ended with a winner in the finals of majors. These are the best players in the world and over 67% of all points played in these finals ended in errors.

Match	Total Points	Total Winners	Winner %
2010 Australian Open Federer d Murray	216	71	32%
2010 French Open Nadal d Soderling	181	55	30%
2010 Wimbledon Nadal d Berdych	171	56	32%
2010 French Open Soderling d Federer	245	69	28%
2010 Australian Open Federer d Tsonga	139	52	37%
2010 Australian Open Federer d Hewitt	179	39	21%
2009 French Open Soderling d Nadal	271	80	29%
TOTAL	1850	564	30%

Stretching wide

Two-handers are never more vulnerable than when they are pulled wide on a serve or a volley. Most adult amateurs are not able to generate sufficient torque from that position (as tempted as they are to try once they see Nadal, Murray, Sharapova, et al pull it off). But if they were to release one hand, everything about the stroke and their body positioning would change. They have more balance, they can reach further, and with only the one hand on the grip, it naturally turns palm down, thereby opening the face of the frame. Instant slice. Now they have a chance to lob, chip, or stab their way back into the point.

The gold standard

Roger Federer's one-handed backhand is a portrait of harmony and balance. Most players accomplished with one-handers use their off hand for balance, as Federer is doing here.

Charging a serve

It is easier to hit a slice backhand while moving forward than it is to hit a topspin backhand. Topspin backhands require good preparation, more windup, better timing, and clean footwork. Slice backhands, on the other hand, call for an open face, involve a descending swing plane, and if I'm being honest, allow for lazier footwork (good slices are hit while running through the shot). Also, the slice is not hit as hard, does not travel through the air as quickly, and therefore gives you more time to get into an aggressive volleying position.

Defending against the lob

The sleeper virtue of the slice is what it can do against a baseline lobber. You no doubt have encountered the opponent who is content to hang on the baseline and throw up an endless procession of defensive lobs. You can identify the situation by your clear preference for having your eyes gouged out rather than finishing the match. Win or lose, you end up feeling tortured by her (or him, but let's be real, the legends in this trade are lob queens). She takes your hardest hit balls and blithely throws them up in the sky, using minimal effort and imparting maximum frustration.

But if you hit a heavy slice against her, the ball is going to stay low, not convert to topspin after the bounce, probably skid, and above all, tend to descend (not ascend) off of her racquet. In other words, she'll have to work harder for her height, the likely result being more overheads for your side.

It happened on court

My partner and I were once the benefactors of the slice-as-weapon tactic when it became clear to us that our opponent had no idea why the ball was careening down off of his racquet. It started with our returns of serve on second-serve points in which he chose to stay back. Most of his forehand drives (and he had a good one) were finding the top of the net and it left him confounded. Then my partner tossed in a few heavy slices against his advances to the net. There, the effect was even more pronounced as he was taking the ball out of the air. Sure enough, his volleys were all coming off his strings with lower trajectories than if we had hit topspin, and he couldn't understand why he was netting so many. His response was to blame his strings and change racquets.

The final straw came on an overhead that found the middle of the net. At this point, he accused the tennis balls (which we had provided, as the home team) of being defective and wondered out loud if we had done this intentionally. We assured him that we did no such thing and invited him to open up a fresh can of his own. We stopped short of suggesting that he watch a Ken Rosewall video.

♦

You do not have to abandon your two-hander to hit a slice. You can open the face and swing high to low with two hands. I don't think it is as easy, and it doesn't address the problems of being taken wide, but if you are wedded to two hands, that doesn't mean you cannot incorporate a slice.

My final thought on this subject is to challenge the notion that you become wedded to two hands in the first place. If you served with two hands and hit your forehand with two hands, then perhaps you could sell me on it. But two-handers remove their top hand all the time and the more comfortable they get doing it, the more versatile their games will become.

7

The Art of the Poach

If there is a signature chapter in this book, this is the one. And if a signature move were to be assigned to me, it would be the poach—the move across the net to intercept a ball intended for your partner's side of the court. Few aspects of the game can be more unsettling to opponents, and not coincidentally, few things on the court will feel as satisfying.

Poaching can be a real game-changer. It can be as dangerous as the more conventional weapons of big serves and aggressive returns. I suspect that my ability to intercept returns and groundstrokes is worth a half-point on the NTRP scale. Without it, I'd probably be a 4.0 player. And across these next several pages, I will risk whatever advantage I might enjoy in league play by sharing every single one of my secrets and inner-most thoughts about why, how, and when I choose to cross. After having revealed all of my secrets, we'll see if any of my USTA captains still want me on their teams.

When to cross

It is probably too simplistic to say that you should cross anytime you think you can win a point. (I'm really giving away those secrets, aren't I?) It also wouldn't be entirely accurate, as I will sometimes cross when I don't think I have much of a chance of winning the point. I also refute that the best time to cross is when you think it might surprise the opponent. I would rather my opponent be of the belief that I will *always* cross (more on that soon).

Like most players, I am more comfortable crossing when my forehand volley is in the middle of the court, and as a left-hander, I enjoy the advantage of that being the ad court. It is those 40-30 and ad-in points where I am most apt to move.

And when I poach, I start by watching, not the ball, but my opponent's front shoulder, because that will provide the first clue as to whether he or she is going to try to hit behind me. (Let's assume I'm going up against a man here, just for pronoun simplicity, and let's assume he is right-handed and playing the ad court.) His feet could tip me off, also, and many experienced poachers prefer to watch the feet, but I find his shoulder to be a bigger and easier-to-watch target. If he keeps his shoulder closed on a forehand return, odds are he is directing his return crosscourt. Conversely, if he has opened his shoulder a bit on a backhand return, I'm suspecting crosscourt and sniffing a green light. In the deuce court, it would be the opposite: closed shoulder on a backhand return is go time.

Where	Cue	Conclusion
Deuce Court	Closed stance on forehand	Could go down my line
	Open stance on forehand	Probably hitting crosscourt
	Closed stance on backhand	Probably hitting crosscourt
	Open stance on backhand	Could go down my line
Ad Court	Open stance on forehand	Could go down my line
	Closed stance on forehand	Probably hitting crosscourt
	Open stance on backhand	Probably hitting crosscourt
	Closed stance on backhand	Could go down my line

These aren't absolutes, of course, and I've been fooled countless times by returners who can conceal their intentions. But it is nonetheless one of the first things I look for in my search for cues that might tell me about return direction.

More important than the position of his shoulders is the position of the serve, and that's why poaching is a team effort: the more my partner can serve middle, the more dangerous I become at the net. Remember Axiom No. 1: good doubles is won by taking away the middle of the court. With a partner's good deep serve down the middle, I can begin moving before my opponent has made contact with the ball, and then there is practically no crosscourt return that I can't reach. That means his only recourse is to try to pass me down the line, and that's advantage us. (He might succeed—perhaps more than once. Stay tuned for why that is a good thing, not a bad thing.)

Green light special

If you are the server's partner, with your forehand volley in the middle of the court, you should be foaming at the mouth when you see a first serve hit like this. Imagine what your opponent would have to do, especially if right-handed, to get this ball away from you.

If I have gotten the cue and the conditions are right, I want to start my move about a quarter-second before my opponent contacts the ball. In that interval, there is time for him to become distracted by me but not sufficient time for him to redirect his return behind me. That's a lot of things that have to happen in a very short space of time:

- Serve lands in the court.

- Opponent prepares to hit return.

- I receive a positive cue from his body.

- I move to poach.

- He hits return.

All of that takes place in about a half-second—less for a big, flat first serve—so the recognition and reactions have to become instinctual. In fact, this is the first time that I have actually tried to describe in words how I respond to a potential poach, and as I read it back, it sounds impossible. Stay tuned for Poaching 1A and how you can ease into the experience.

There are two exceptions to the timing of a poach:

A planned cross, where my partner is covering behind me and I am responsible for any crosscourt return, including a sharp angle into the alley. For that, I leave as the serve bounces. We'll discuss the pros and cons of signaling soon.

A kamikaze move, where my partner's second serve lands so short in the court that we're about to get eaten for lunch. If I move really early, I might distract my opponent, might provoke him to change his return, or I might get lucky and get my racquet on the ball. I might also get pasted, so this move is to be used with caution.

I don't always get my cues from the position of the receiver; sometimes I just feel that the conditions are right. The score, the pattern of previous points, my opponent's returning style—they all add up to tell me that he or she is returning crosscourt and it's a good time for me to go.

Poaching 1A

If you want to add the poach to your game, there are several things you can do to ease into it, and this first piece of advice is the easiest one of all to follow: stand in the right place!

It astounds me how protective people are over their alleys, to the degree that they have taken themselves out of the point before it has even started. Is this you, in the diagram below? Did you get passed once in 1978 and it has scarred you for life, to the point that your sole purpose as the server's partner is to insure against anyone ever winning a point down your line?

Stop doing that!

Get out into the middle of your service box where you belong so you become noticed by your opponents and so you can be in a position to help your partner. See the "Getting Passed" section coming up soon.

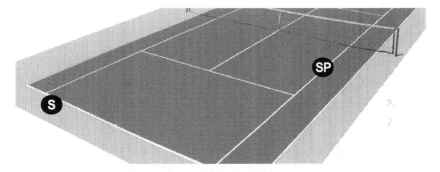

Done before you've even started

Net players who over-protect their alleys do their partners no favors. You should start the point in the center and the middle of your service box.

Most of us did not learn how to hit a volley while moving laterally, so that might be a new skill for you. As you learn it, you will frame many volleys, so you must separate the experiences of crossing and of volleying. You might cross well but blow the volley, so don't get discouraged.

The best conditions for poaching exist when an opponent's weaker wing is down the middle of the court on the side of your forehand volley. In the following diagram (next page), let's assume that the right-handed receiver in the deuce court does not have a strong backhand. And you, the right-handed server's partner, can cross into the middle with your forehand volley. This is go time for you and stands as an excellent opportunity to practice.

I also suggest that you try baby poaches, where you take one or two steps to the middle on every serve, without committing to the actual cross. If the return is weak, then you can go after it. If not, you stay on your side. You can repeat this for the duration of the point, too, always taking those couple of steps to the middle each time the opponent hits crosscourt. That helps you groove the good habit of looking middleward.

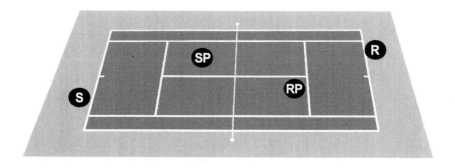

Weak backhand? Green light!

If you know that your partner is going to serve middle to an opponent's weak backhand, you should be ready to cross on just about anything you can reach.

Don't keep score by how many winners you record, and please don't obsess over getting passed down your line. Just try to get comfortable with the timing and the meter of the cross and with hitting volleys on the move.

Your target

Remember the discussion in Part One about how the crosscourt stroke is to be hit deep? Well, this is the exact opposite. When you cross, your target is right in front of you: the shoetops of the receiver's partner (position a in the following diagram). You are not trying to hit her; you are just trying to reduce or eliminate any chance of the ball being returned.

If you aim for the middle of the court (position b), you give both opponents a chance of getting a racquet on the ball. And if you aim for the alley to your opponent's left (c), you become vulnerable to a lucky guess and a winner down your alley. Focusing tighter, hitting to her waist gives her a chance to hit a reflex volley and bouncing it in front of her offers her a half-volley. But the shin and ankle area? Almost indefensible.

I am not suggesting that positions b and c are bad; you are still in a strong position to win the point. Your goal, however, should be position a. Furthermore, the closer you are able to get to the net, the more dangerous you are and the more options you have. From there, you could angle the volley to either alley with much less risk of it being returned or you could bounce the ball over both players' heads.

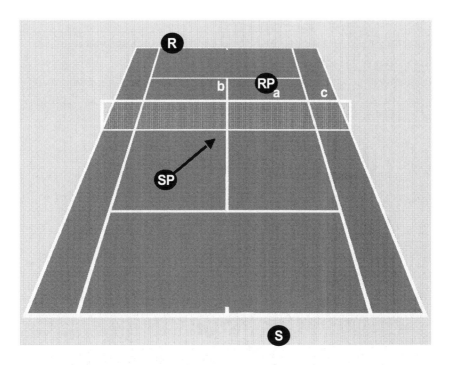

Position A

The best place to hit a volley on a poach is at the ankles of the receiver's partner. You still keep control of the point with a volley down the middle (b), but you increase the chance that an opponent retrieves it. And volleys into the alleys (c) put you at risk of losing the point to a lucky reaction.

This is why the best poachers move diagonally to the ball, in the hopes of intercepting it right at the net cord. And in turn, this is why experienced poachers do not start by crowding the net. Not only does that potentially tip off the opponents, but it makes for more challenging geometry. While you would think that the best route would be the shortest distance between the two points, it is actually easier to start a bit further from the net and move diagonally toward the net. Forward movement is good for any volley and is the secret sauce for a poach. So even though you hope to end up right on top of it, don't hug the net in your ready position.

Getting passed

Now we come to what might be the most misunderstood idea of all: the specter of being passed down your line when you cross. I have watched hundreds of volleyers freak out from getting passed once and render themselves utterly ineffectual for the remainder of the match. Has this happened to you? As if the receiver has humiliated you or insulted your manhood?

Please.

If you become active at the net, your opponents will try to hit behind you and they will succeed from time to time. That is to be expected. It is not to be feared. In fact, it is not even a bad thing; I would argue that it is a good thing. You *want* them trying to do that. It takes them out of their more comfortable crosscourt rhythm, and more important, it's hard to do! Returning down the line is a low-percentage play—the net is higher there and the geometry is more challenging.

The worst thing you could possibly do is stop crossing because you were passed once. That is the only way your opponents can claim a victory from the tactic. If I had to quantify it (and this is another first for me, as I have never thought it through to this extent), I would say that an opponent would have to pass me at least six times in a match to compel me to stop crossing. Did I say in a match? Make that in a set.

In fact, I'll go even further here: I not only want my opponent to try to pass me, I want her to succeed. (Notice that I have switched pronouns here, just to clarify that good net play knows no gender.) If she succeeds in passing me, she will likely assume that she has put me in my place (literally), and can now resume crosscourt returns. And now I have the upper hand, because I am not going to curtail my crosses.

The best time to cross is right after my opponent has tried to pass me, irrespective of whether she succeeds. And the best situation of all is when an opponent tries to hit behind me several times and fails and then finally connects with one. I will make a point of complimenting the shot. "That's too good," I'll usually say. "I did not think that you could thread that needle."

That's what I say; here is what I hope she hears in her head: "Okay, you just tried four times to pass me and you failed. You finally made one and that shows both of us how hard it is. You know it, I know it, and you know that I know it. Now that we both know your success rate, 1 for 5, I'm going to move more than ever and you're going to have to do way better than 1 for 5 to stop me."

An untold number of instructional books will speak to the value of the down-the-line return because it will "keep him honest." That only succeeds if you allow it to. I'm here to tell you that all of those books are wrong. Do not allow a pass attempt to keep you honest; view it as an invitation to cross more often. (So why even try to return down the line? See the end of this chapter.)

Against players with really good returns of serve, this ends up being quite the cat-and-mouse game, and much of my thinking (and in some ways the muse for this book) was shaped by practice matches with my friend Jim Horen. An excellent defensive player with an impossible-to-read return, Jim could return down my line almost at will, especially in mixed doubles, when he has a bit more time to set up on the return. He really does keep me honest and our practice sets typically feature 15 to 20 pass attempts off of serve.

It's all a chess game, as we each try to determine the likelihood of poaches and pass attempts. And I made the mistake of proclaiming one day, "the best time for me to poach is right after you've returned down the line," because now he knows my tendencies, and I know that he knows, and he knows that I know that…okay, you get the idea.

Jim has been good for my game because he has reminded me that it's not a trauma to be passed and it is not a reason to stop crossing.

Going further

Here is a collection of other semi-random thoughts about poaching. You can tell it is my favorite topic, yes?

Should you signal?

This question often boils down to personal preference. Some partnerships like to know what each player is doing and others don't want to clutter their heads with it. My moves are instinctual and spontaneous, and when I signal to my serving partner, I lose a bit of that spontaneity. On the other hand, if we are struggling to hold serve, we need to confer more often and might then actively plan things, including crosses. If you and your partner choose to signal, here are some thoughts:

- Make them simple. The standard closed fist for staying and open hand for going works just fine.

■ You both have obligations. If you say you're going to cross, your partner needs to serve middle.

■ Agree on what happens if your partner's serve inadvertently goes wide (but still in). Will you still go or is the cross now off?

■ If you signal that you're staying, it should be understood what you are really saying is: "I'm not committing to a cross and you shouldn't cover behind me, but if I think I can pick off the return, I'm going."

■ Servers should not reveal a cross by changing positions behind the baseline, or worse, by serving and then dashing across the baseline to cover the other side. Not only does that tip your hand, it makes for serves that land short. Make your first step into the court, so you don't cheat your service motion, and then cut across.

■ Agree on whether a cross is just the first serve or for both serves. Second serves can be good times to cross because few people expect it.

Head fakes? Nah...

A favorite practice among net players is the early move to the center with the hope of distracting the receiver or trying to draw his fire. When you employ a head fake, you make an early and pronounced move to the middle of the court, as if you are going to cross, and on contact, you return to your original position. If the receiver tries to return behind you, you are there to respond to it.

This might be a perfectly credible tactic but it does not help the poacher in any way. In fact, it hurts him. A head fake involves negative motion—when the receiver contacts the ball, you are moving back toward the alley, not toward the middle. You are ceding ground, not seizing it, and as such, it has nothing to do with poaching.

When I see opponents employ head fakes, it emboldens me. The sudden, almost jerky, move toward the center is unmistakable and when I see it, I know that my opponent has just taken himself out of the play. I can hit any old crosscourt return.

Cheating toward the middle as your opponent returns is not a bad move, but don't think of it as a fake—think of it as early preparation. Early movement makes you more responsive, more ready to move in either direction. But you're not faking—you are not indulging in the exaggerated move in one direction, to be followed by an equally out-of-proportion move back. Cheating involves small steps; head fakes usually involve big steps.

Second serves? Yah...

Unless your opponents are pummeling your partner's second serve, this is a great time to cross. Why? Because very few people do it! Opponents are expecting to be able to hit a simple crosscourt return without worrying about you. Perfect time to go, IMHO...

Surprise? Overrated

Many point to the element of surprise as being an important poaching quality. I don't. I want my opponents to know that I will always cross on any ball that I think I can reach. Implicit in a surprise attack is the notion that the opponents were not expecting it or were not thinking about it. I want my opponents to always be suspecting that I will go.

If I surprise my opponent with a poach, the implication is that he could have defended against it had he known. If I successfully poach when he knows that I might go, that's more powerful. It essentially says to him, "You knew I was going and you still couldn't do anything about it. You can make bank that I'm going the next time, too."

Poaching against the serve

One of the most powerful tactics you can employ is the poach as the returning team, where serving teams feel that they have an advantage and you take that advantage from them. Here is the typical situation, employed most often in men's doubles, where the likelihood is higher that the server advances to the net. It's a second serve and you are anticipating a shallow serve to be hit to your partner, whom you hope returns crosscourt. Right after you see the serve bounce (you can't shirk your responsibility to call the serve in or long), you shift your focus to the oncoming server. If he begins to bend at the waist and/or the knees, you know that your partner succeeded in both hitting crosscourt and getting the return low. That means the resultant volley or half-volley is going to be traveling from low to high. That's your cue: begin your cheat to the center as soon as the ball passes the net player, ready to assault the net as soon as the server volleys. As you can see from this diagram, the server is not in a very good position to direct his volley to your alley; this is total go-time.

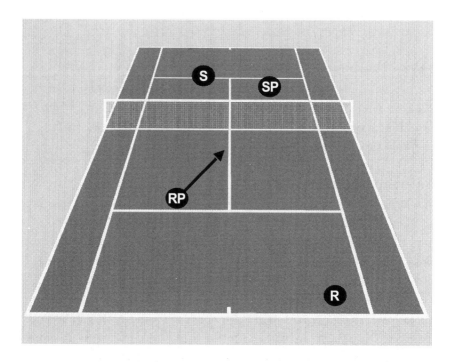

The poach on return

If your partner gets the return low and crosscourt, get on your horse. Yes, the server could flip a volley into your alley, but the likelihood of success is low. Wouldn't it be great if your opponents tried 10 times to do it in your match against them?

You must make sure not to leave too early; you must make sure that the server's partner is not also poaching. If he is, you have become his sitting duck with no time to react in defense. I haven't been injured much on the court, but the two times that come to memory are when I moved too early on a return poach and put myself directly in the line of fire from a conventional poach. Again, this move is best done on a second serve when the likelihood is higher that the receiver can hit a firm crosscourt return, low and away from the net person.

The other thing I watch for is if the oncoming server is using his inside wing to volley—right-handed backhand volley from the deuce court or right-handed forehand volley from the ad—because those are the most likely positions from which he will volley crosscourt.

While I don't signal much as the server's partner, I will almost always tell my partner that I plan to cross on his return. I want him to be ready to cover my vacated court and I want him to hit crosscourt. This is not to say that I won't cross without signaling; I want to reward any good return that I can. I make the distinction between a response in the moment and a premeditated and unconditional cross. In the case of the latter, I always tell my partner. Similarly, if we had planned for a cross but my returning partner's instincts tell him to crack a ball down the line, no harm done. He reacted in the moment to a cue he received.

It happened on court: success at Stanford

One of my favorite recent memories came at district playoffs for 9.0 mixed, where my partner Lien and I were underdogs against Dan, a 5.0 player and former teammate of ours, and his partner Holly, able to play as a 4.0 despite her recent move up to 4.5. We stole the first set against this 9.5 team, got hammered in the second set, and were holding our own in a third-set supertiebreaker. This was taking place at Stanford's Taube Stadium with about 300 onlookers, including at least 50 with vested interests: our teammates, our opponents' teammates, and two other teams, whose chances for advancement rested on the outcome of our match.

With the match in the balance, Dan showed his first signs of nerves with a double fault serving to Lien while ahead 8-7. He then netted a first volley to give us match point at 9-8. Lien is now serving in the ad court to Dan.

So let's assess. With the match on his racquet, he double faults while serving to the woman, enroute to losing both of his service points. Now facing match point, what are the chances that he is going to return down my line? Zero! My direction to Lien was concise: "Serve middle." His safe return cleared the net by about three feet and I had moved so early that I arrived at the ball in time to bounce it off the court and over the fence. That victory earned us a trip to sectional playoffs.

I don't tell that story merely to brag (okay, maybe a little—it was a great moment), but to suggest to you that as you incorporate the poach into your standard arsenal, you will become more confident with the move, perhaps to the point that you consider it a high-percentage shot. Neither one of us, Dan nor I, wanted to make an error on this critical point, so we both employed what we considered to be low-risk shots. I have been hitting forehand volleys on the run like that for so long, it has become second nature. It was literally the highest percentage play to make.

It's a good feeling when you regard a shot as high percentage that most others identify as risky and improbable. You can have that feeling, too.

Defending against the poach

If this chapter has given you the impression that there is no defense against the poach, well, that's a good thing for us poachers. The best defense against my poaching your return is not necessarily for you to try to go down my alley but to meet the return early and take my time away. The older I get, the more difficult it is to track the ball off of your racquet, and if you move in, you make everything happen even quicker.

The happy irony here is that you might find that this makes you a better returner, and I discuss this in detail in Chapter 17. Stepping in takes your own time away, too, but that might actually work in your favor, as you might find yourself turning your brain off and hitting more instinctually. The most challenging returners to poach against are the ones who say, "screw it, let him poach if he wants. I'm just going to crack this return an inch from the net and we'll see how he handles it."

I know from my own experience that my best returns often come when I am moving forward and playing with a bit of abandon. In those situations, I don't try to place the return so I don't actually know where it is going. I just know that if I make good contact, there will be a lot of pace, a fair amount of topspin, and it will be low to the net. All good things.

Finally, I wouldn't want to give you the impression that it is always a bad idea to return down my line. But don't do it solely as a response to my movement; do it because you are good at it. If you love hitting crosscourt backhand returns and you're in the deuce court, it's simply good strategy to take a few of them down my line, whether or not I cross.

If you can establish that you have a reliable down-the-line return, that is a weapon that I have to contend with. And if you take the ball early and show that you are willing to crack returns— *"who cares where they go, as long as I smack them!"*—you tell me that you are a dangerous player.

When to change strategy (and when not to)

8

wo years ago we won the first set 6-1 by pounding deuce-court serves down the middle at our right-handed opponent's weak backhand and devouring his weak returns. They began the second set by switching sides, where now his weak backhand was out wide (not our preferred serving location) and from where he could poke lobs over the alley and stay in points. They pushed us to a second-set tiebreaker, largely on the strength of that strategic shift.

In 2009, after double faulting across nearly two entire games, a server alternated between serving at the center T and serving from the furthest point allowable, at the outside edge of the doubles alley.

Once in 2010, after losing the first set, a team played the entire rest of the match in I-formation.

Last year, I encountered an opponent who switched from righty to lefty in the middle of the match.

And once, about 15 years ago, an opponent tied a balloon to her shoe-lace. Yes, on a string! We were never sure exactly why, but we did hear her say to her partner, who was as mystified as we, "I can't possibly play any worse." My partner was about to check if it was legal and then turned to me and said, "Wait, why would I want her to take it off?" Good point.

Indeed, tennis lore is graced (or littered, depending upon your point of view) with stories of people who changed strategies mid-match, sometimes in the name of strategy, other times out of desperation, and occasionally for the sake of folly (like the time that an opponent chose to serve from five feet behind the baseline, after being called for two consecutive foot faults).

So let's start the conversation by pointing out the obvious. You should consider a change in strategy if you think it will give your side a better chance at:

- Utilizing a weapon of yours

- Exposing a weakness of theirs

- Disrupting their flow

- Messing with their minds

The success of the change needs to be measured in net gain, because most strategic shifts result in some compromise to your own play (otherwise, you would have done that in the first place, right?). And while I am never an advocate of raw gamesmanship for the sole purpose of destroying an opponent's frame of mind, I acknowledge that a good strategic shift could have that as a byproduct.

In broad strokes, you would consider a strategy change if you are having trouble holding serve or breaking serve. I like breaking it down this way because it shifts the focus away from whether you are winning or losing. I'm not convinced that "because we're losing" should be the sole criterion for changing strategies. If you are holding serve with ease but missing 3 out of 4 serve returns, you're not losing but you sure as hell are doing something wrong. And because most of us compartmentalize our games down these lines, you could make a change to your serve or your return strategy without it disrupting the other.

If you are getting outplayed in the normal course of a point, outside of serve or receive, that is more worrisome, because you have to contemplate a shift that would change the nature of how you play every point. But before we go climb any ladders, let's consider our lower-lying fruit.

On serve

If you are having trouble holding serve, play more I-formation (where both you and your partner start from the middle of the court, one of you to cover in one direction and the other going in the opposite direction). We'll discuss this in detail in Chapter 15, but to cut right to the chase, it is easier to serve middle from that position, and anytime you can attack the middle of the court, good things could happen. And if you want an even simpler argument for I-formation, most people simply serve better from the middle of the court.

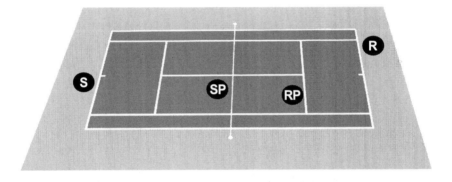

Quite the panacea

Most players see results from I-formation simply because servers serve better from there.

We can (and will, in Chapter 14) discuss the various types of serves you could consider hitting, but I'm not sure that the middle of a match is the best place to start hitting kick serves if you don't actually own one. But serving out of the "I" can help your serve no matter what type of serve it is.

On return

While servers initiate, receivers react, and that adds a challenge to any discussion of improving your fortunes. (And once again I'm going to refer you elsewhere, Chapter 17, for deeper discussions on the return game.) If you're looking for a cure-all for return issues, the one to try first is to the take the ball sooner, as discussed at the close of the previous chapter. No matter which side, no matter what type of serve, meeting it earlier could change everything. You make it harder for the net person to poach, you make it harder for the server to close on the net, you increase the likelihood of opponents having to hit up on their first volley instead of down, and you create possibilities for angles that might not have existed otherwise.

I'm not suggesting that you actively try to do any of those four things (defeat the poach, preempt the close, make them hit up, create angles), and that perhaps is the biggest benefit of all in moving in on returns: you no longer have time to think! Missing returns can mess with your head and the best thing you can do to combat that is to turn off your brain. But the last time you checked, it didn't have an off switch. Hitting aggressive returns is the closest you might get to finding an off switch, because you make everything happen in an instant.

Now I don't want you to put yourself in harm's way, so if you are getting blasted off the court by a big server, don't do this. In fact, do the opposite: stand five feet behind the baseline and throw every return up in the air, as high as you can and as deep as you can. That gives you the best possible chance at getting the ball in play while also changing the rhythm of the point.

Are you surrendering?

Moving off the baseline to receive serve is a concession. You could argue that any strategic change is a concession; it's all Plan B, otherwise, you would have done that from the outset.

Yes, you are telling your opponents that you can't handle what they are dishing out and I suppose that could embolden them or give them cause to think you have become intimidated.

Build a bridge and get over it. The only thing that matters is changing a result; disregard everything else. You are problem-solving and in so doing you are exhibiting some of the best qualities that competitive athletes can possess: flexibility and creativity. In fact, I would argue that showing the willingness to change could send a more powerful message to your opponents than anything else that could be inferred from a strategy shift.

It happened on court

It's really easy to get carried away with implications and inferences. I once watched a pair of my teammates win the first set and then change their strategy and start lobbing because they were convinced that their opponents were going to start rushing the net. Their opponents did no such thing and won the final two sets when our team lost its way amid their new lobbing campaign.

◆

Change your strategy if you think that your current direction has little or no chance for success. That is the primary criterion. Keep reading, though, for a bit of gray area.

When not to change it up

In my experience, partnerships change their strategies when they shouldn't at least as often as do they refuse to make a change when they should. Here's the scene: You have just lost the first set 6-3 on one early break and five easy holds by the opponents. You only reached 30-30 or deuce against serve twice while you had to fend off continual challenges on your own serves.

You didn't play badly at all, serving no doubles, returning with a high percentage, making most of your first volleys, and committing few unforced errors. And the last time you faced this team, you won in straight sets. But this time, your opponents have simply been unconscious and that makes you feel helpless as you sit down for the changeover before beginning the second set.

What would you say to your partner? What advice would you offer to change your fortune? You might be able to uncover a legitimate strategy shift that could stem the tide, but I want to suggest something different, if for no other reason than because so many teams fail to consider it.

Stay the course.

Let's look at the facts here. You and your partner are playing well and you know that you are not overmatched, given that you won against this team in the past. You are serving well, returning well, and not making sloppy mistakes. There is nothing obvious to point to that you can or should be doing better; you're just being outplayed. Sure, you could try stuff, but that carries with it just as high of a probability that it will mess you up than it will mess them up. Ask yourself two questions:

- Can we continue to play at this level?

- Can they continue to play at this level?

If you think that your opponents' level of play is not sustainable, your best course of action would be to force them to keep playing that well in order to win. If they are unable to, that giant sucking sound you will hear is momentum rushing to your side, because you are in the perfect position to seize control of the match. You remained patient, you didn't panic, and now you need only continue to play the way you have been in order to gain the upper hand. Once the magic runs out, it is likely to be they who will start changing things, pressing, and battling their collective patience.

Let's make one change to this fictitious set that you lost. What if your 6-3 loss included two breaks of serve, a flurry of errors, lousy returns, and an 0-3 statistic on break points? Now should you change your strategy?

No, you should simply play better. Shore up your returns, don't make stupid errors, focus better on break points. There is no reason to change your game if you haven't yet played your game! Now if there is something preventing you from playing better—the sun, the wind, an injury, a hangover—that might be different. A change might give you the jolt needed to overcome what ails you.

◆

If I were to sum up this entire discussion about contemplating a strategic shift, I would do it with five questions to ask:

- Are you losing?

- Could you play better?

- Would changing your strategy result in your playing better?

- Would it result in their playing worse?

- Might they start playing worse without your doing anything?

It happened on court

My partner Elaine and I were playing an 8.0 match two seasons ago against a strong 4.5 guy and a steady 3.5 gal. The match was very close but we discovered early on that the guy, playing the ad court, either had a bad backhand return or was just having a bad day with that stroke. As his misses piled up, I encouraged Elaine to set up wider than usual to help her steer as many serves as possible to his backhand. Finally, during an ad-in point midway through the second set, he connected with one and drilled a winner right down the middle of our court, leaving both of us surprised and flat-footed.

We lost the deuce point also, and Elaine approached me to talk. "Should we serve to his forehand this time?" I didn't remember the colorful phrase that I used in response, but Elaine reminded me of it for the rest of the season.

"Are you on crack?" I allegedly replied. He is batting less than .100 from his backhand side, he hits one lucky winner, and my partner wants to change course. "No way!" I told her, "make him do it again." She did, he framed a ball into the side fence, and then proceeded to smack his racquet into that same innocent fence.

Moral of this story: don't overreact to a great shot by your opponents. It's only great if they can do it over and over again, otherwise it's lucky. An opponent who relies on luck, well, that's my kind of opponent.

All About Partnerships

If the world were perfect, your organized team would be comprised of people with the ideal mix of personality, temperament, and playing style. Team chemistry would be overflowing, and for every new player brought aboard, the perfect partner for that player would be found.

Isn't there an app for this?

In our less-than-perfect world, we have to work a bit harder at finding a good partner and being a good partner. Developing the right brew of style and substance takes time, patience, and experience, but it will be time and effort well spent, whether you are seeking a partner for yourself or whether you are a team captain trying to create the best combinations. A good partnership is a joy to behold, and I'm here to tell you that it is not just a roll of the dice. You can make it happen, and this part of the book explores how. Many of the thoughts here are written as much for team captains as for players.

9

Choosing a Partner

On most of the teams I play on, teams are formed almost by accident. Your captain has announced a Tuesday night practice session and you are one of four people to show up. "Okay, let's see...Rick, you play with Ken, and Bill, you and Nick play." Are Ken and I right for each other? What if I'd rather play with Nick? Am I going to say anything? I don't want to hurt anyone's feelings.

Was more than a millisecond of thought put into this? I'm not here to cast any aspersions on the wonderful people who captain teams. They are heroes for their willingness to take on a role that I would not accept, and if I did, I'd be terrible at it. It's just not realistic to expect that captains can treat this like Davis Cup, pouring over statistics, mulling over combinations, obsessing about relative strengths and options. (Some do, and they deserve awards. Most can't.)

You should therefore regard it as your responsibility to consider who might make a good partner for you. Your captain will likely appreciate the help and thank you for the input. Unless, of course, you just looked for the best player on the team and said "I want him." No, you need to put some thought into this. Here are the things you might want to think about.

Born to lead

Are you the take-charge kind of guy or gal on the court? Do you naturally tend to direct the action? There's nothing wrong with being a headstrong player, but what if you are paired with another headstrong player? Is that twice as good or is that a train wreck about to happen? I have seen plenty of partnerships comprised of two headstrong players and know many who have enjoyed tremendous success as a team. The key is not that one of them suppresses ego and attitude and allows the other to be the boss. The key is that both players become good listeners.

It sounds simple, but it's not. What do two born leaders do when they have no followers? You need to ensure that each of you is a sounding board for the other. When your partner suggests that you play I-formation in the ad court *and* serve out wide, you must resist the urge to respond with how ridiculous you think that is.

I remember the following exchange on a mixed doubles team I was on between two very headstrong players:

"I think you need to lob more."

"No, she'll just cream anything I throw up there."

"Well, we have to do something, because she's creaming everything now."

"We need to get the ball away from her forehand."

"Let's try the lob."

"So lob to the backhand? Lob right down the middle?" [She was in the deuce court.]

"It's worth a try. Now, the guy's overhead is right there, so we might just be trading one poison for another."

"He's not quick enough to get back for them. What kind of a backhand do you think she'll hit?"

"Let's be ready for a floater. Hit kind of a line drive lob and then let's go into I."

"Okay. If she can angle a high backhand volley, she deserves the point."

Not only was the strategy brilliant and helped them to a come-from-behind win, it was an excellent example of effective problem solving during a changeover. You can see that each acted impulsively at first—*that idea's no good, mine is better*—but when they started actively listening, their ideas became greater than the sum of their parts. They agreed to try to find her backhand, incorporated the idea of the lob, and game-planned around the type of response they predicted she would have.

Now, it doesn't always work out this well. I have an equal number of memories of times when egos clashed, communication suffered, and resentment prevailed. *"Sure, whatever. We can try that for now, I guess."* Not the most supportive environment, eh?

I'm not exactly a shrinking violet on the court, but I once played an entire season with someone who made me feel that way. His name was Jamie, he too was left-handed, and he fit all of the definitions of a hothead. He expected to make every shot, ordered me around the court, would make only weak attempts to hide his displeasure over my errors, and would fire balls in anger over his own mistakes. This was many years ago, but I still remember one of his anger shots, because it hit the scorekeeping unit on the net post and pieces of shattered plastic rained down on the court. I was embarrassed and often made to feel uncomfortable by his on-court attitude.

Did I mention that we went undefeated for an entire season?

For all of his boorish and demeaning behavior, when Jamie asked for my opinion about strategy, he would usually incorporate it into his own thinking. He would act as if it were his own idea and would continue bossing me around the court, but our awkward collaboration worked, to my complete surprise.

Two strong court presences can enjoy success. They just need to learn to listen.

Born to follow

What about the opposite situation—the player who is passive by nature and more comfortable being directed? Some of my favorite partners of all time were very quiet on the court, needing serenity to play at their best. (Don't pair them with Jamie!) You want to provide them with the court environment they need, but at the same time, there is such a thing as having too much calm. You must have passion in order to play your best, and if passivity reigns over the court, where does that passion come from?

This played out for me in one of my most memorable losses ever. My partner, Andrea, was a wonderful player (still is, I'm sure, although this was over 10 years ago), but she was having a bad day. She struggled with nearly every phase of the game that day, and yet we still battled our way to a match point in the second set, on her serve. I crossed and drilled a volley right at the hip of our opponent, an excellent 5.0 woman with great hands. I think the ball hit her racquet three times in her desperation scoop-lob, and the dead quail that landed back on our side so surprised us that we lost the point. Our opponents won that game, won the next two games to win the second set, and ultimately, the match in three. (To this day, I wonder what the result would have been had I been able to follow my advice in Chapter 7 and get that volley at shin level.)

Andrea was a quiet player, an excellent athlete, and a thinker. Through her struggles, I was as supportive as I knew how to be, never showing exasperation, always offering encouragement, and often laughing along with her over the uncharacteristic errors she was making.

I thought I was doing the right thing, until I received an email from her that night. "You made me feel so comfortable today, I think maybe I was too comfortable." In other words, I was being too supportive; she might have preferred that I grab her by the shoulders and yell "what's the matter with you??" I wanted calm on the court and worked hard to create a supportive environment, especially in mixed. Andrea needed anything but calm; she needed me to create a bit of turbulence for her, but I didn't recognize that.

Perhaps in retrospect, Andrea and I were not a good emotional match. And at the same time, I went undefeated with hothead Jamie? Who could possibly figure all this stuff out??

Fire, all the time

If two passive players run the risk of not finding their passion, what about matching two players who wear their passion on their sleeves? I've been on the short end plenty of times against players who practically worked themselves into a frenzy, but I've also witnessed my share of total flameouts. The one I remember in particular was from a mixed doubles match back in the 1990s in which I had the privilege of playing with Sue Anawalt, doubles champion many times over and member of the Bay Area Tennis Hall of Fame. We were playing an away match against a husband-and-wife team, both of whom were playing out of their minds and at a fever pitch. High fives after every winner, evoking and encouraging lots of cheering from their supporters, shouting encouragement between each point.

They were doing nothing that violated the rules, nor were they being unsportsmanlike, but at 5-1 down in the first set, I wanted to throw something at them. Sue could sense my frustration, and simply said, "Be patient—they can't keep it up."

"They don't show any signs of slowing down," I replied.

"When the fire goes out, it will be out for good."

Sue was right; their emotional pitch was unsustainable, and when it started to wane, they had nothing to fall back on. With the drop in the emotional energy level came a noticeable drop in performance and then in confidence. The crowd fell silent and we rolled, 7-5, 6-1.

I touched upon this back in Chapter 8 and I'll talk more about this in Chapter 24, when we seek the true meaning of confidence. What our opponents showed that day wasn't it. Being on fire or being in the zone isn't the same thing as being truly confident. Confidence is sustainable and can survive emotional peaks and valleys. Teams that rely on passion need to be able to weather the breaks; in fact, they need to learn to create emotional breaks for themselves so that they don't flame out. The best competitors learn how to channel and control intensity, and you can usually recognize them by the following qualities:

- They walk slowly between points.

- They hold their racquets in their off hand before each point.

- They don't celebrate wildly over points won.

- They seem to have just as much energy two hours in as when they started the match.

I coach girls softball, where these young athletes are just starting to learn about these concepts. I give them a very simple exercise. "Clench your fist," I tell them, "and keep it clenched." After five seconds, when they inevitably loosen their grip a bit, I admonish them "Did I tell you to stop? I didn't tell you to relax!"

They then tighten up with renewed vigor...which lasts all of another five seconds. They quickly learn that intensity is not a commodity that can be sustained over long periods. In order to have intensity, you must also have un-intensity.

The best athletes understand this and use it to their advantage. They explode with intensity for the duration of a point...and then they become as relaxed as they can be...until they prepare for the next point...and their energy gradually builds...until the ball is put in play...at which point they explode all over again.

◆

This discussion about personality types and emotional pairings is fascinating to me, but just how useful is it? Can you really choose a partner based on your emotional compatibility, and if you could, does that mean you should? Or is it better to make this determination based on playing styles?

If left to the ethereal qualities of our personalities, I surely would have rejected playing an entire season with Jamie. He drove me crazy but man, were we good! When we were both at the net, we felt like nobody could ever get a ball past us or over us. I'm not sure that I have said two words to him since that season—we were not destined to be friends—but we created a partnership that worked.

In that regard, doubles pairing is not unlike dating: you are first attracted to someone's looks and physical features, and then you determine if you are compatible on emotional, psychological, and spiritual levels. Let the forehands and backhands attract you initially; then determine if you are compatible on deeper levels. So maybe I'm writing these two chapters in reverse, but it's my book and I'll write backwards if I want to...

10

Matching Playing Styles

Let's continue our dating analogy: Having a successful partnership in tennis requires more than swiping left or right on Tinder. As tempting as it might be, it's not enough to watch a dude with a huge serve or a gal with an amazing backhand and proclaim that you have found your partner. Apart from chemistry and personality, what makes for a good match?

Do opposites attract?

As in life itself, some of the best partnerships I have seen have matched up players with completely different styles, and that is often my first criterion when sizing up opponents or evaluating potential partnerships.

Let's take the guy with the huge serve and monster forehand. What happens if you pair him with another big hitter? When they're on, watch out, you could get hurt as their opponents. But if they go off the rails, who puts them back on track? This is why I like to see big hitters teamed with players with good hands, as each of them can effectively end points for the other and they will be more likely to create a balance of intensity.

I am certainly in the latter category here—all hands and feet, no power—and some of my favorite partners have been guys who can put a hurt on the ball. The critical quality is actually more specific than big hitting: can they force guys to hit up from the front court? If they have to hit up, I can hit down. That's a pretty simple formula that has worked for decades: my partner makes them hit up so I can hit down.

On the ladies' side, a similar dynamic can exist between a steady baseliner and a partner who is comfortable moving at the net. As a strong groundstroker, you might be able to hold your own against most opponents, but imagine how effective it would be if your partner were able to cross and pick off a few of those crosscourts? Now your opponent has to worry about being bled to death and think about your partner at the net.

It happened on court

Proof that quality trumps quantity, in the 2012 Australian Open, the team of Sania Mirza and Elena Vesnina upset the No. 2 seeds Lisa Raymond and Liezel Huber, winning a third-set tiebreaker, 8-6. At 7-7 in that breaker, Mirza was eight or nine strokes into an intense rally when Vesnina crossed. Apologies to historians if I have these partners mixed up—I channel surfed to the Tennis Channel just in time to watch the last 15 minutes and I didn't know either player. Her winning volley was notable for two reasons: 1) it was astonishingly easy, and that was because 2) according to the announcers, it was the only poach she attempted in the entire third set.

This fascinated me—so much so, in fact, that I went to the tournament's website in hopes of watching a press conference or reading more about this. And sure enough, in the transcript of an interview, a journalist asked Vesnina (again, I think it was Vesnina; it might have been Mirza) why she waited so long into the match to move at the net.

Her reply, translated into English: "If I had done it earlier, it wouldn't have been as effective."

Talk about good timing! This is about as opposite as you can get from my own kamikaze approach to net play that I share in Chapter 7. She saved this move until the point where she needed it the most. After two hours of relative passivity, her opponents were completely unprepared for the move.

Brilliant.

Ask not what your partner can do for you...

The final thoughts of this chapter go to Jon Toney, one of my playing editors, who offers a wonderfully-different take on the question of effective partnerships.

> The question for me about my partner is not what type of player I'm looking for in a partner but what type of player I need to be. It starts with being more selfless. Singles is all about selfishness, but doubles is about selflessness. Look at John McEnroe: frequently a self-absorbed jerk in singles, but a great team player in doubles.
>
> Selflessness extends to strategy, as well. Can my serve and return set my partners up for winners? And what to say when they set me up? "Great shot, partner!" might come the comment from my partner, to which I invariably respond, "Great job setting me up."
>
> Finally, we win or lose as a team. If we find ourselves explaining losses with "Jon was a bit off today, or Rick was not at his best today," then we are off track as a partnership. When my partner and I lose a close match, no matter how well I played, there are always some shots I'd like to have again. And sometimes losing simply meant my opponents played better.
>
> A bit like life itself, if I'm thinking about how I can make things better for my partner, then I'm a pretty decent partner. If instead I'm obsessed with searching for and finding the best possible partner, I would do well with some earnest introspection.

Choosing Sides

It might remain an eternally open question. Which factors and qualities are more important: the ethereal ones discussed in the previous chapter or the more pragmatic ones in this chapter? What I find fascinating about the topics here in Chapter 11 are that each one could completely contradict another. I am reminded of a skit in the old I Love Lucy show (and no, I'm not quite old enough to have watched it when it first aired). Ricky is trying to teach Lucy to play golf and he peppers her with a variety of fundamentals. "Watch the ball…keep your left elbow straight…bend your knees…relax your wrist…feet slightly open…weight over your front foot."

She honors each piece of advice to the letter and adds it on top of the others until she resembles a tortured pretzel.

Don't become a pretzel: the thoughts in this chapter are designed to be digested independently of one another. Any one of them might resonate with you, but if you tried to incorporate all of them at once, well…#basketcase.

Pretty good chance you'll find something to relate to in this chapter. Everyone has a forehand and a backhand and everyone is either right- or left-handed. If that's not the case—if you have an "other" to share—I'll give you an entire chapter in the next edition.

Comfort is king

Let's cut directly to the chase, shall we? If you are decidedly more comfortable on one side or the other, play there, end of discussion. Few factors can trump comfort, in my view, as that will translate directly into performance, especially at playing levels below 4.0. At 4-4, 30-30, you don't want to be saying to yourself, "I'm really an ad court player...I hope I can get this serve back." There are better conversations to have with yourself, like how you have already hit 30 backhand returns and you are completely prepared to hit one more. Or how you might not be sure if she is serving middle or wide, but you've been creeping inside the baseline all afternoon and you are prepared to spring in either direction. Or simply how you are totally ready to take the serve early and hit your return on the rise.

So the question of comfort is tantamount. But I want to risk a bit of analysis (as in "paralysis of analysis") because it would behoove you to explore why you are more comfortable on one side or the other. I'd like you to go beyond a simple acknowledgment that you prefer one thing over another. That kind of discovery could make you a more versatile partner.

The classic example is the right-hander who likes to hit crosscourt backhands from the ad court. That shot has comfort written all over it, and if this is your stroke we are talking about, you don't need a whole lot of exploration to know that you just like it. But if we dissect it a bit, we are likely to come up with tangible reasons why: the ball travels over the shorter part of the net, the diagonal angle gives you the most court to hit into, and right-handed opponents at the net are not as likely to poach against it.

If conditions demanded that you play the deuce court, you would lose a lot of your warm and fuzzies, as you would face the specter of hitting a more difficult "inside out" crosscourt backhand (defined by a racquet motion that has your hands closer to your body on the backswing than on the followthrough) and you would have to do that against a potentially more menacing opponent at the net by virtue of a right-hander's forehand volley being in the middle.

But if you thought about it, you might have the following conversation with yourself: "I love ripping my backhand from the ad court...what if I made that same swing here in the deuce court? What if I went right at the net person? The net is higher there, but I have pretty good clearance on the shot. And while the court isn't as long down the line, I hit with enough topspin. After a few attempts, I bet I'd become nearly as confident with it on the deuce side as I am on the ad side. I'm not going to try to hit winners; I'm just going to hit down the line and see what happens. And my partner has her forehand in the middle—maybe she could cross and pick off a few floaters."

Exploring your strengths allows you to go off auto-pilot and that is usually healthy. The standard move here would be to steer backhand returns back to the server, and if you're on auto-pilot, you might not think past that. (After all, I devoted the entire first chapter to the value of hitting crosscourt.) But if you don't own that shot, not only might your returns be weak but they are more likely to fold under pressure. If you understand with a bit more depth what you like about your backhand, you create more options for yourself. You might always prefer hitting backhands from the ad court, but now you won't have to fear playing the deuce court.

This became relevant for me when I explored my tendency to lob more from the deuce court than in the ad court. I figured it was simply that it was easier to lob when taken wide, but that wasn't it. In the deuce court, my lobs travel over two backhands when playing against right-handers, while on the ad side, lobs over forehands can be met with a crueler fate. As soon as I got a clue about this, I realized that a crosscourt lob from the ad court not only crosses backhands but also creates a potentially awkward response as opponents have to adjust to an unfamiliar angle.

My forehand is bigger than your forehand

For a majority of players in our ranks, the forehand stands as the stroke that can do the most damage, either on a return or in a rally. Therefore, it makes sense to look there first when discussing big shots. If you love to wind up and blast forehands, while your partner is particularly adept at hitting inside-out, you have a clear path: you head to the deuce court and your partner plays ad, where each of you can hit your preferred strokes. This is particularly true at playing levels below 4.5.

Of course, this approach is rendered completely moot by opponents who can serve to your backhands, so this strategy, like just about every other one in this book, can't live in a vacuum. For every player who believes you should play to your strengths, I'll find you a player who believes you are only as good as your weakest shot. So let's offer up a slightly different formula for choosing sides:

- Put the steady player in the deuce court

- Put the big hitter in the ad court

Assuming right-handedness, this allows the deuce player to set up the ad player on balls hit in the middle of the court and it encourages the ad player to go for big returns on pressure points. With the ad court player's forehand on the inside, you will also be encouraging him or her to take more of the overheads. In the absence of prevailing factors, this positioning is worth a try.

Granted, you can formulate the exact opposite argument. You could make a compelling case for wanting to have the steady and more reliable player taking returns on those big ad-court points. Google steady and "deuce court" to find enough opinions to write a short book on this topic alone.

Mental sturdiness is certainly a factor in all of this, but I don't find a strong enough correlation between *steadiness* and *sturdiness* to generalize. I've seen as many big-time chokes among steady players as I have among big hitters. In fact, if my partner is choking, the first piece of advice I'm usually going to offer is to "relax and hit the crap out of the ball." In pressure situations, I'd rather have my partner swinging harder, not softer. So when you add it all up:

- Forehand volley and overhead in the middle

- Big points call for big weapons

- Know which strokes stand up better under pressure

It suggests that you at least try this formation in practice matches. I also like to turn the entire conversation inside-out and suggest that the side you play can and should dictate the style of play you adopt. If you are not known necessarily as a steady player or a big hitter, allow your side to influence the way you play. In the deuce court, think about getting as many balls back as you can and giving your partner opportunities to end points. And if you are in the ad court, look for opportunities to rip forehand returns up the middle and backhand returns crosscourt as you move to take over the middle of the court.

The mixed doubles conundrum

Adding the mix of genders to the discussion creates a delicious blend of herbs and spices. Mixed doubles not only widens the gap of relative playing strengths, it generally introduces a different playing style, as women tend to stay back after serves and returns more often than do men. Mixed doubles also encourages an additional strategy, as opponents might choose to hit at the woman instead of hitting crosscourt.

At playing levels below 8.0, it all gets back to the point made at the outset of this chapter: where are you most comfortable? Letting players play to their strengths and in their comfort zones should prevail over just about every other factor in the lower playing levels. Are you more solid off the forehand than the backhand? Do you consider your crosscourt forehand a weapon? Do you actually like to volley or do you just do it when required? These are going to be the most relevant questions for mixed doubles at the lower playing levels. So:

- If the right-handed guy is effective at cutting off volleys, put him in the ad court.

- If the gal has a strong two-handed backhand, place her in the ad court.

- If either player has a really weak backhand, try to hide it in the deuce court, where it is not as easy for right-handed servers to find it.

Any one of these factors could be enough to drive your decision on side at playing levels below 8.0. At the higher levels, however, the situation could change profoundly. It is not uncommon at the 8.0 level to see a 4.5 guy playing against a 3.5 woman. That is a large gap, too large to ignore when planning strategy. Ditto for the 9.0 level, where 5.0 guys could be squaring off against 4.0 women. In those situations, if the woman is in the ad court, expect the guy to serve a big kick out wide to her backhand. She'll spend the next two hours fielding serves bouncing high and away from her, and whether she hits with one hand or two, she will be in for an exhausting ordeal.

And at the 8.0 and 9.0 level, you won't be able to hide a weak backhand, as players serve middle with higher accuracy. In both of these situations, your key to survival will be to take the ball earlier (a tall order with the ad serve out wide) and/or to become one with the lob. Or hit several thousand backhand returns in practice and simply raise your proficiency and confidence with the stroke. What a concept…to work on a stroke…

In all of these cases, the key to thriving in mixed doubles is flexibility. The better teams find a way to compensate for the gap in playing levels with a willingness to adjust (usually in the middle of the match) to conditions that could otherwise work against them.

Damn lefties…

At a minimum, righty-lefty teams in any type of doubles—men's, women's, or mixed—need never worry about serving into the sun, as one of them will always be able to find a place to toss on the sunny side. Beyond that, however, little is clear as there is no unanimity of thought on how to approach the question of side choice.

Let's start with a maxim that holds true to this book's core philosophies. Then I'll let you pick it apart.

> With a left- and a right-hander, it's best to place forehands in the middle of the court. So play the left-hander in the deuce court.

In this position, either player will have a better chance of taking control of the middle of the court. There will always be a forehand volley at the net strap and an overhead covering the middle of the court. And depending upon foot speed, both alleys will be covered as well, as each player can cross to cover lobs into alleys. A case in point is the cover of this book, in which U.S. Open finalists Santiago Gonzalez and Abigail Spears are both right-handers. She will have to back-pedal aggressively to hit an overhead, but that might be preferred to whatever high backhand Gonzalez will have to attempt.

In the absence of other factors, forehands up the middle is what I normally suggest and the conversation usually takes a familiar pattern:

Me: Do you have a preference on side?

Him: No, I'm fine either way.

Me: Well, if you really have no preference, then I would-

Him: Wait, you're a lefty, aren't you? We should put you in the ad court then.

Me: If you prefer playing on the deuce side, then yes we should play that way. But if you truly have no preference, I would suggest we put our forehands in the middle.

Him: I thought that lefties always play the ad side.

Me: And I thought that righties actually used their brains once in a while.

No, I have never actually made that last remark (nothing like insulting 90% of my readership all at once). But I do find it amusing how right-handers react to us. First off, they rarely notice during warmup that we are left-handed (I've played singles matches where we're six games into the first set before my opponent has noticed), and then when they do, they go on auto-pilot right away: *oh, well, you should go play in the ad court.*

There are plenty of reasons why that might be the best course of action, but *because you just should* will never be one of them. Here is a smattering of responses to this question of how and why a lefty-righty partnership should line up.

From Bob in Bloomington IL

Usually 3.0 servers and below will place most serves to the outside of the service box. Assuming players are stronger to their forehand, this would imply that the lefty play the ad court and the righty play the deuce court. As the servers get better (3.5 and definitely by 4.0) they are more likely to be able to hit consistently to the returner's backhand.

From Jason in Boca Raton FL

Regardless of the stronger player, the lefty in the ad side and the righty on the deuce side allows the doubles team to cover more court on wide serves, angled returns and angled rally shots. They will also provide better court coverage when their opponents have opened the court with any of the above shots.

From Bill
in
Walnut Creek CA

I disagree with the idea of playing a bookend pair with all the firepower kept in the middle. I am a 3.5 player, and my partner and I (both righties) recently demolished a very strong 3.5 pair (6-1, 6-1) who used exactly the proposed alignment. This pair both had great forehand skills, which we recognized early. After a few probing games in the first set that were actually fairly close, we began to serve to the outside and return their serves to the far side of the court. We effectively neutralized their net game (by staying away from the middle), and, by playing our strong forehands against their backhands, we forced them to make weak returns that our net player consistently jumped on.

I feel that we could have lost this match if we had been matched forehand to forehand, as their forehands were that much better than ours. I was amazed that they failed to change this in the second set, but the left-handed player was clearly the boss and not inclined to give up the deuce side. I vote for lefties on the left!

From Mike
in
Topeka KS

I'm a 4.0 doubles player, and when I play against a team that has a lefty-righty combo, I always hope the lefty is in the deuce court, unless he has a really strong backhand.

I can easily serve to his backhand in the deuce court using my slice serve and often pull him fairly wide. The shots that follow the serve I'll hit cross-court to his backhand, which has the virtue of being away from his net partner. His cross-court returns usually come to my forehand, so it ends up my forehand against his backhand, a situation that I like. Also, slicing into his body on his forehand side is easier in the deuce court and is an effective serve because, if he tries to move to his right to hit a forehand, the ball breaks in the same direction, often jamming him.

When the lefty plays the ad court, it is more difficult to serve to the backhand. The shots after serve are difficult to hit to his backhand, as well, if his partner at net is at all active taking away the middle. Any shot directed to the backhand of a lefty in the ad court has to go through the middle, close to the net man. It then ends up being my backhand vs. his forehand, which usually isn't a good situation for me. I often go to the Australian formation when playing a lefty in the ad court for this reason.

◆

These comments suggest what we already knew: there are no absolutes in these decisions. But for every one of these comments suggesting forehands outside, I could have cited three that argued for the opposite. I don't place a lot of stock in the notion that left-handers are vulnerable to the wide serve in the deuce court, for the simple reason that we lefties have been facing right-handers pounding serves at our backhands or swinging us wide for decades. If we can't handle that, we're playing the wrong sport!

If I need to, I'll pull out the ultimate trump card. The Bryan brothers used to play with lefty Bob in the ad court but switched about five years ago and have since become the most dominant and successful partnership in men's doubles history.

In general, we southpaws feel as if we have a half-of-a-pawn advantage in most matches. Right-handers don't have to face us very often, few below the 4.0 level have actively game-planned against us (and as mentioned earlier, sometimes they don't even notice), and those who do will inevitably become a bit more mechanical in their thinking.

Furthermore, and this is the one generalization that I do subscribe to, we lefties have been dealing with a right-handed world our whole lives, and that makes us more adaptable. We learn to use scissors with our right hands, deal with the three rings of a binder being where our writing hand wants to be, find the seat at the table where we are least apt to bang elbows with our neighbor, and discover ways to move more quickly and efficiently to our backhand side on the court.

This is not enough to overcome superior talent—if you are better than I, you will beat me most of the time. As I said—perhaps a half of a pawn. But like a blackjack player, I can recognize when the deck is stacked in our favor, and one of those times is when I serve in the deuce court with a right-handed partner and a right-handed opponent with a suspect backhand. I will cheat a bit to the middle to more readily find the backhand and I will inform my partner to try to poach on anything possible. Furthermore, I will tell my partner, guy or gal, to close aggressively on the net and not worry at all about the lob. With my overhead on that side, I can cover anything that goes up. This combination of factors becomes lethal.

Add it all up and this much is clear: a lefty-righty partnership has a lot of opportunity to explore and exploit. If done effectively, this team can do well together.

Playing against left-handers

Of the many rewards of authoring this book, this next section does not promise to be one of them for me. But I've given away all of my other secrets, so why should this one be any different? Would it be lame if I told you that we lefties face lefties just as infrequently as you do, and that I am therefore unqualified to comment?

I didn't think that you would buy that one, but I am still going to defer, as playing editor Jon Toney has given this more and better thought than I have. If you charge me with copping out—that I just can't bring myself to do it—I will plead no contest. Here's Jon...

> When Rick asked me to write a section on playing left-handers, I told him that I consider myself an expert at losing to them. He regarded that as neither an acceptable credential nor a reason to decline, so either way, the assignment is mine.

> My main thoughts on playing southpaws boils down to serve and serve return. If the left-hander is predominantly a slice server (many of them are), I try to hit backhand returns, because if I move to the forehand side, the serve is going to follow me and I'm going to get jammed. And if they can reverse kick the serve the other way, I can usually tell by he ball toss. So first order of business: prepare to hit a lot of backhand returns.

> When serving, it depends what side the left-hander is playing. In the deuce court, I'm going to serve wide and into the body and I'm going to keep doing it until it won't work any longer. In the ad court, I will almost always play I-formation to force the lefty to hit backhands to my forehand. As Rick has pointed out, in the end, talent will prevail, but I'm going to make the left-hander demonstrate that his or her backhand is better than my forehand.

The 2014 women's final at Wimbledon was a case study of what a great lefty server can do. Eugenie Bouchard entered the final being anointed as the next great champion, having not dropped a set, and yet was completely dismantled by Petra Kvitova. Which brings up my final piece of advice: If you know you are playing a left-hander, practice against a good one today!

◆

Okay there...are you happy??

12

How to be Your Captain's BFF

Earning playing time on a USTA or club team involves many variables, not the least of which might be how quickly you respond to your email. ("We need a gal for tonight—first one to reply gets it!") Honorable captains look beyond sheer talent as they try to even out playing time and still be competitive. They also have the important requirement of making sure that players qualify for a hopeful post-season by playing in the minimum number of matches required for eligibility. If you take it all into account—aptitude, availability, compatibility, eligibility—captains have a big job on their hands.

What can you do to increase your chance of playing regularly on your team? Yes, hitting a 120mph serve would be a good place to start, as would a lights-out overhead and killer mid-court swinging volley. But we live in the real world, where you probably own exactly none of those strokes.

Absent said serve, overhead, and swinging volley, here are a few things that players of either gender at any level can do to increase the chances that their captain will ping their email address the week before the next match.

Play either side

We just spent a few dozen pages together exploring how to make the best choice of sides for a partnership. From that discussion, I hope that you don't develop such a strong opinion that you become rigid in your thinking. Few things are more frustrating to a captain than having to sift through conflicting requirements of side. Similarly, few qualities are more valuable in good doubles than flexibility and versatility.

This versatility begins with your ability to play either side of a doubles court and I want you to start by answering this rhetorical question: Is it okay for you to pay lip service to the idea and say "yes, I can play ad," when you don't really mean it?

Yes it is. It is okay to say that. That's how versatility is born. There might not be a player on the planet who can truly say that he or she is equally comfortable on either side, ad or deuce. In our heart of hearts, we all have a preference. So you must begin by fooling yourself and making yourself believe that you really can play equally well on each side. And the way to believe it is to say it, out loud. I'll go first:

I like playing the deuce court because I can lob over backhands and I can hit forehand volleys from the middle of the court. I feel like I can take over the match from the deuce court, so I'll take that side anytime.

I really like the ad court because I can hit rolling forehands for winners and chip my backhand at the feet of volleyers. And I like being the guy on critical ad-in and ad-out points. So give me the ad court anytime.

Can you tell which of these statements more accurately portrays my beliefs? Even if you know me and have played with me, I would defy you to tell me which I believe in more. I don't think that even I could tell you: I have been sharing these sentiments for so long, I no longer know which applies to me more. I might have a preference, but I don't actually know if I am better on the side that I prefer.

You can do the same. List three or four reasons why you would enjoy playing your non-preferred side and say them out loud. Say them in conversations with teammates or over a post-match beer or wine. And make sure your captain hears you.

More important, when the time comes for you to play that side, remember those reasons and try to implement them. They become your blueprint for playing that side.

Now this isn't a magic wand—you won't overnight become as capable or as confident on your off side. But it will help you get there; it will help you become more comfortable on that side when the need arises. And that will improve your value to the team.

This approach is the opposite of conventional thinking that suggests that the more you do it, the more you earn the right to say you can do it. I submit that the more you say it, the more capable you become at doing it. If this is too much psychobabble for you, just allow room for the possibility that there is a symbiotic relationship that exists between saying it, believing it, and being able to do it. And once again, I will refer you to Chapter 23 and the discussion about lying to yourself.

The answer, my friend, is playing in the wind

Few variables are more potentially frustrating than playing on windy days, and you have probably heard it said that the wind can be the great equalizer, allowing a weaker team to hang with a stronger one.

Bullsh*t!

The wind isn't the equalizer here; a bad attitudes is. Players who blame losses on the wind are just as apt to attribute lost matches to mysterious injuries, a bad string job, music playing too loudly from a nearby park, or their cat, who needed a shampoo on the Tuesday night when a practice match was scheduled.

Do you really want to be that person who seems never able to play to potential because of some outside influence? Do you think that will go over well with your captain? Wouldn't you rather be the person who doesn't get bothered by factors outside of your control and who relishes the opportunity to take on a challenge, any challenge? How you handle the wind says a lot about you as a come-ready-to-play teammate.

Unless you ball-toss like Steffi Graf or take backswings like Gustavo Kuerten, playing in the wind is mostly a mental challenge. It's harder to time the ball, it's a guessing game trying to anticipate the bounce, it's tricky to predict the spin, and if you're human, all of this weighs on you.

The wind should be seen as an impediment to performance if it blows only on your side of the court. The wind is an opportunity to show opponents that you handle obstacles better than they do. Consider the following statements:

The wind won't bother me nearly as much as it will my opponents because I hit a lot of volleys, which are easier to hit in the wind than groundstrokes.

The wind is not a problem at all because my serve returns have a lot of topspin, allowing them to penetrate the wind.

I am going to enjoy this wind because it will make it impossible for the opponents to lob.

This wind is going to work to my advantage because my lobs will flutter around, creating havoc for anyone who tries to hit overheads or other aggressive shots.

Do you notice how the last two statements are self contradictory? That doesn't matter; the only thing that matters is that you embrace them, contradictions and all. The wind is merely a mental challenge and that is an opportunity to show your mental fortitude.

About five years ago, our 9.0 team moved from an indoor club to outdoor courts and I earned the reputation of being the "wind guy." Anytime it was windy, I would publicly celebrate and spout some proclamation similar to the ones above. My reputation even migrated to opposing teams who came to the belief that I was a dangerous player in the wind.

This was terrific…except there was absolutely no basis in actual fact. There is nothing about my playing style or my physical stature that should result in a tangible advantage in windy conditions. But I celebrated my affinity for it so much that everyone else came to believe it. That made it real, and to this day, were you and I to step out onto the court, I would be of the belief that I would handle the wind better than you.

Show me the lights

I am intimately familiar with this topic. I am ideally credentialed to speak with authority on the challenges of playing nighttime tennis, as I most likely have the worst uncorrected vision of anyone you will ever know (-14 in my left eye, for those scoring at home). I praise daily the entire opthalmic industry for having created contact lenses, but as I age, my eyes are clearly becoming the organs that are deteriorating the most rapidly. And that makes tennis under the lights supremely challenging.

I can't tell you that I have spun it all the way into a positive the way I have with the wind, but I have learned how to survive in the nighttime sky by taking note of the one positive that it brings to the court.

Total focus.

Playing at night offers the near-total absence of visual distractions away from the court. No planes flying overhead, no cars driving nearby, no kids playing soccer in the adjacent field. All you see is the court. (In my case, I don't even see the ball half the time, but now we're getting off track.)

This focus makes it easier to watch the ball hit my opponents' strings, which for me is huge, because the reduced lighting makes that same task *harder*. I'm able to process opponents' movements better and dial into the drama of court positioning.

None of this makes me a better player under the lights because I start with a big deficit. But it allows me to survive at night, and most of you who don't walk out there half-blind can use these same techniques to truly thrive under the lights.

Give me anybody!

To go full circle on our discussion about partnerships, expressing a willingness to play with anybody will help your stock with your team captain and make you more flexible and versatile. The lobber…the basher…the loud mouth…the hothead…the guy who questions line calls…the gal who makes questionable line calls. You don't care—you'll find a way to inspire anyone and bring out the best in a partner. What an awesome ability to have and to put on display! And if you don't actually feel it, that's okay—put it on display anyway.

◆

I'm not yet blue in the face, so I'll keep saying it: with matters of the heart and the mind, your belief in a certain situation is the most important component. Believing in it can make it true, and sometimes just saying it, even if you don't believe it, can turn it into reality.

Serving and Returning

If the service ace is akin to a home run, a return winner is like a diving catch in the outfield. Both can make you feel great and both can be overrated. If you can hold serve with regularity you become difficult to beat, but if you can't break serve, you had better learn to love the tiebreaker.

This section is a collection of thoughts that could help you think just a little bit different about the two signature activities in the sport you love to play.

13

Is it Better to Give Than to Receive?

How many of you go on auto-pilot when you win the toss and immediately proclaim "We'll serve"? I know how prevalent that is because I do it myself, often against my own best interest. In his popular book *Winning Ugly*, Brad Gilbert argues that amateurs should choose to receive almost always, as more service breaks occur in the first game of a match than any other time.

I'm not sure if Gilbert has statistics to back up that assertion (which he made in the 1990s), but my own experience certainly bears it out. Early service breaks in the opening set are standard fare at all of the levels I play, and I feel most vulnerable in my first one or two service games.

And let's be fastidious about this because you don't just choose serve or receive. When you win a toss, you get one of three choices:

- To choose to serve or to receive

- To choose to begin on one side or the other

- To designate that the other team chooses first

Up with pacifism

Two significant factors in all of this are the location of the sun and the possibility, especially in mixed, of one partner being a more powerful server than the other. While it is simple to establish that one player on your team will always serve first in a match or a set, it is not quite as simple to orchestrate on which side that player begins. That is why the passive choices are often good, especially the choice to have the other team pick first.

Let's create a scenario. It's 11:00 on a July morning and the sun is high in the sky. Jamie and Jordan are playing against Chris and Casey in a match that could be men's, women's, or mixed, involving players of any NTRP rating from 3.0 to 5.0. As they are warming up, Jamie notes that the sun is exactly where the toss would go but Jordan tosses a bit over the shoulder and could serve on the sunnier side. Their serves are generally equal in strength and it is not particularly important who serves first.

Meanwhile, on the other side, Chris is the better server and would normally be the first to serve for that team, but Casey is left-handed and can easily avoid the sun.

Jamie and Jordan have a fairly simple task: have Jordan serve on the sunny side, whether serving first or second for the team. But for Chris and Casey, the situation is not as easily orchestrated: how can they ensure that Chris serves first and on the non-sunny side?

Thanks to the miracle of modern graphics, the diagram on the next page is rendered from the opposite side of the sun, so enjoy this once-in-a-lifetime perspective.

Choices, choices

On this sunny day, there is a lot to consider among these two teams with different priorities and serving strengths.

Let's consider the possibilities:

Jamie and Jordan win the toss and choose to serve: Chris and Casey would choose to start on the sunny side so that Chris could then serve first on the non-sunny side.

Jamie and Jordan win the toss and choose to receive: Chris and Casey would choose the non-sunny side so that Chris could serve first.

Jamie and Jordan win the toss and choose the non-sunny side: Chris and Casey would choose to receive, so that their first service game, after the changeover, would be on the non-sunny side.

Jamie and Jordan win the toss and choose the sunny side: Chris and Casey would choose to serve, so that Chris could start straight away.

So if the team of Jamie and Jordan win the toss, Chris and Casey will be able to orchestrate the situation to their satisfaction. They might not be serving the very first game of the match, but they will be ensuring something that is arguably more important: having Chris serve first and from the preferred side.

Ironically, they might not enjoy the same advantage if they were to win the toss. Watch:

Chris and Casey win the toss and choose to serve: Jamie and Jordan choose the non-sunny side and so if Chris is to serve first, it will have to be into the sun. It would be better for Casey to serve first on that side but that would be a strategic concession.

Chris and Casey win the toss and choose to receive: Jamie and Jordan choose the sunny side, meaning that after the change, Chris would have to serve into the sun. This would be the worse decision for them as they give up serving first and end up on the less-preferred side.

Chris and Casey win the toss and choose the non-sunny side: Jamie and Jordan could choose to serve first and once again, after the changeover, Chris and Casey are hosed.

Chris and Casey win the toss and choose the sunny side: Jamie and Jordan could choose to receive, forcing Chris and Casey to serve first into the sun.

So when they win the toss and choose first, Chris and Casey place themselves at the mercy of their opponents. That said, Jamie and Jordan have their own agenda; they're not just trying to foil Chris and Casey. So in some of the scenarios above, their choices will work out for Chris and Casey. But the only way for Chris and Casey to guarantee their preferred arrangement is when Jamie and Jordan choose first.

That is why the "make them go first" choice is often a good idea if you win the toss. You should consider it when your team has needs or preferences beyond simply serving first.

I'm sure I have a few of you shaking your heads over how complicated I have made this, and indeed, players with big serves would roll their eyes at all of this nonsense. "Just give me the balls so I can serve, okay?" was how one player put it when his partner overanalyzed this after winning the toss. What a great problem to have that your serve is so imposing that you render all other considerations moot. Most of us don't have that problem. Most of us need all the help we can get with these things.

I also don't mean to dismiss the value of being one game ahead throughout a set. If you can receive at 3-4, 4-5, and 5-6 in a close set, that is pressure your opponents feel and you don't. If you are confident in your abilities to hold serve, you should choose to serve and disregard all other factors. But in the real world, it rarely works that way, and so knowing all of your options is helpful.

It happened on court
Years ago (okay, decades ago), my regular partner was also left-handed, and his name was also Rick. We once played a match at Golden Gate Park in San Francisco, with a troubling sun and a stiff wind. It was the finals of a doubles tournament and many of our friends stuck around to watch. The sun was the issue for us and our opponents were talking about whom they wanted to have serve against the wind. We won the toss and my partner spoke for us.

Rick: We'd like you to choose first.

Them: We'll choose that side.

Rick: We'll choose to receive.

At Golden Gate Park, spectators are very close to the court, and one of our friends couldn't help himself. "Wimps," he shouted across the court for all to hear, while everyone around laughed. Indeed, it might have been the most passive selection of serve and side in history.

Serve first or volley first

An additional consideration is the player who helps a team more by volleying at the net than by serving from the baseline. I am that person and I create interesting dilemmas for my mixed doubles partnerships. With a less-than-overwhelming serve, I probably do not hold serve at the same percentage as most men do. On the other hand, my woman partners likely hold serve at a percentage higher than most other women because I help them out at the net a lot.

Once again, the moral of the story is clear: don't go on auto-pilot! You might have perfectly good reasons for staying the traditional course, choosing to serve first, and having the guy serve first in mixed. I just want you to know what those reasons are and know what your options are.

That's what makes doubles more fun than singles—all of the options to consider and variations of play that are possible. That is part of the joy of contemplation and it is also one of the reasons why I don't recommend that you take this book out onto the court with you—this is a read best read while you are imagining things, not trying to actually practice them.

14

The Most Important Quality of a Serve

I remember it like it was yesterday, even though it was actually nearly 30 years ago. I was taking the written test as part of a quest to join the United States Professional Tennis Association. The USPTA was (and still is) the most prominent governing body of teaching pros in the country. I did not aspire to be a tennis teacher, but many of my friends and colleagues were, and while at *Inside Tennis*, I worked closely with them on articles I wrote and events that I attended. So it seemed like a good idea to earn the credential and I actually crammed for the test with Keith, a buddy who taught at a Marin County club. Here was one of the multiple choice questions:

Which of the following is the most important quality of a serve:

a) Pace
b) Depth
c) Placement
d) Spin

How would you answer that question? I'll tell you which answer the USPTA deemed to be correct later in this chapter, but first I'm going to be coy and argue on behalf of each answer.

Pace

Few things are more effective than hitting big serves. When you can earn a free point on every service game, you will be very tough to break. And if you can hit big serves, you don't even have to worry about placing them—it's just bombs away and let's hope your opponent doesn't get hurt. Indeed, not only can a big serve earn you cheap points, it can also intimidate opponents. Two wins for the price of one.

Depth

If you can consistently hit serves close to the service line, little else matters. Opponents have less time to react and they cannot step into the court to hit returns. The servers who can serve deep with consistency will hold serve just about every time.

Placement

This might be the hardest of all four components to master as serving the ball to different places involves changes in toss, grip, or technique. But those who do it will be considered the best servers around. Nothing is harder on an opponent than having to be ready for serves down the T, out wide, and into the body.

Spin

And finally, the great neutralizer is the serve that cannot be predicted. Like good knuckleball pitchers, often the server doesn't even know where it is going. Slices, kicks, twists—they all play havoc on receivers trying to find their rhythm.

◆

These short write-ups were written with the intent to show no bias toward any one of the four ingredients of a serve. The next section revisits each one, with lots of bias...

How deep is your serve?

The correct answer on the USPTA test was b. Those who hold the game in the highest regard and who devote their livelihoods to teaching it to others believe that the most important quality of a serve is its depth. I agree with this assessment: the best serves hit in amateur tennis are those that land deep in the service box. Your opponents might have excellent reflexes, great two-handed returns, and an ability to pounce on any serve, but until the rules of the game are changed, they must wait for the ball to bounce before they can do anything, and if that bounce takes place at or near the service line, you severely limit the damage that they can do.

The second virtue of the deep serve is that it requires no deception in order to be effective. It doesn't matter if your opponents know you are trying to do it—you could shout your intentions to them if you wanted—there is nothing that they can do to neutralize it.

The final benefit of the deep serve is that it can compensate for a multitude of sins. I might be having a bad serving day—no rhythm, can't place my toss, can't get on top of my serve, no zip on the ball—but I know that I can still be effective if I just find the back of the box. Even if I hit the ball with little pace or spin, my serve can still be effective if it is hit with depth.

My serving partners have heard me say it a thousand times when asked where they should go with a serve on a crucial point. "It doesn't matter," I normally say to them. "Just hit it deep with ¾ pace and whatever kind of spin you want." Depth of serve has no defense and consistently deep serves become fatiguing to opponents.

I also know the converse to be true: if my serves are landing short in the box, little else matters—I'm going to struggle with my serve all day. When this happens to me, it is usually because I allow my toss to drop too low and that is often caused by my failure to keep my head up. So my Rx for this is to remind myself to "climb the ladder"—to not wait for my toss to begin dropping, but to go up and get it. I rarely get to watch my partners serve—I'm always in front of them—but when their serves start hitting the net and landing short, that's the sole piece of advice I offer: go get your toss; don't wait for it to come down.

Fixing other service problems usually requires more aggressive intervention. For instance, if you are not hitting your spots, it could be because you are not pronating enough, or your hips are not at the right angle, or your toss might be in one of about 50 places it shouldn't be. If you are not getting enough spin on the ball, this could be because of your wrist position, or maybe your shoulder, or maybe one of 200 other body parts that is out of whack. And if you lack pace on your serve, that could be due to…well, actually I have no idea why that would be. Maybe the Earth's gravitational axes are off.

Indeed, resolving the other issues of a serve requires tremendous knowledge of your body or requires divine intervention. But if you want to hit your serve deeper, the fix is easy: don't let your toss drop. Climb the ladder and contact the ball at a higher position.

So depth wins for four reasons: 1) It is tremendously effective in neutralizing opponents' returns; 2) it requires no element of surprise; 3) it is the easiest to achieve; and 4) it is the easiest to rescue if it goes off.

Location, location, location

The ultimate endorsement of depth as the most important quality of a serve is that I rank it above placement. After all, I have spent untold number of pages advocating for controlling the middle of the court and for serving middle. How big of a hypocrite can I be??

In fact, I rank placement just a hair behind depth. If you can reliably place your serve out wide, into the body, and (above all) down the middle of the court, you will be very tough to beat. You will frustrate to no end opponents who like to receive serve a step or two behind the baseline, and you will be keeping all but the quickest athletes forever guessing.

At the pro level, placement might be the biggest weapon of all, because from the same toss and same arm motion, the professionals can bust a serve up the middle or hit a serve out wide that bounces in the front half of the service court.

We can't do that and we shouldn't try. Your mission should be to reliably hit three serves: middle, body, wide. Those three serves are different in the deuce and ad courts, so really, we're talking about six serves. Developing that type of proficiency is very difficult to do in matches or even practice sets, but if you can set aside some dedicated time, even 30 minutes, to hit serves, you'll be the better for it.

There are technicians with more knowledge than I who could tell you exactly how to hit each of these serves, but I'd rather you figure it out for yourself. From whatever you identify as your stock serve, pay attention to the adjustment you need to make in order to move your serve around. Do you need to toss the ball in a different spot? Vary your arm angle? Rotate your torso earlier or later?

Start by hitting those spots and tuning in to what you have to do different in order to accomplish it. With practice, you will be able to make those adjustments without thinking about them too much.

With still more practice, you might find that you don't really need that much physical adjustment in order to place your serve. Accomplished servers will tell you that they just think "serve out wide," and that automatically triggers the subtle adjustments necessary. That should be your goal: to place your serve into different parts of the court with minimal physical change to your motion.

None of this is easy, especially at the 3.0 – 4.0 levels, where you feel fortunate to have one serve you can rely on. Now I'm asking you to develop six? The amount of tinkering that is possible could send you to a sanitarium. This is where tennis shares the most similarities with golf, a sport that can send you to the funny farm on a daily basis.

If you reach a level of comfort and want to try out your new serves under match conditions, think first serve. You don't need that kind of stress on your second serve. And at first, the temptation will be strong to patty-cake the serves in order to find those spots. Resist that with all of your might. In fact, try to do the opposite: swing more aggressively and think about imparting more spin on the ball, rather than less.

This is why placement ranks below depth in my view: it is harder to pull off. But if you can start placing your serves reliably, you will be a much better doubles player for it. And if you can blend placement with depth, you could hang with the 5.0s.

To every serve, turn, turn, turn

Third on my list is the type of spin you are able to place on a serve, which is generally greater than on other strokes by virtue of the fact that you have nearly complete control of all variables. Those who know me might be wondering what I'm smoking when I rank spin at three, given that I take full advantage of my left-handedness. If my opponent is not reacting well to my backward ball movement, I'm going to provide a regular dose of it for him or her. And it's usually her—there just aren't that many left-handed women who load the ball up with twist, so most women only see it in mixed, and then only when they play against left-handed men. So we're an oddity to most women playing mixed and I'd be a fool not to take advantage of that.

But I'm the exception, not the rule. Most servers do not regard spin serves as weapons and most opponents don't fear them. At its core, a spin serve is about control, not damage.

Spin Control

The server in the deuce court is hitting a slice that slides after the bounce. The server in the ad court is hitting a twist serve that bounces up and in the opposite direction.

Spin serves come in many varieties, the two most prominent being slices and twists. To hit a slice serve, you would carve around the outside edge of the ball, propelling it forward but with sideways spin. This will not only influence how the ball travels through the air but also what happens after it bounces. In the diagram here (assuming right-handedness), the server in the deuce court is hitting a slice serve. With all of that sidespin, its bounce is going to stay low and continue in the same direction.

The twist serve (or kick serve, as it is also known) involves more body action because you will be imparting sidespin *and* topspin onto the ball.

Your racquet will come up from behind the ball and meet it on the way up. The server in the ad court is hitting a twist and with all of that forward spin, the ball will kick up (hence the other name given to this serve) once it bounces. Depending upon how much you are able to arch your back, a twist serve can actually bounce the opposite way entirely, moving to the left while in the air and then bouncing to the right.

We could split hairs and discuss how the twist and kick are actually different—a twist is a combination of side- and topspin while the kick is pure topspin—but it's largely irrelevant as very few amateurs below 5.0 have enough strength and flexibility to hit a serve with pure topspin. Those of us in the masses between 3.0 and 4.5 are going to approach the ball from an angle when we attempt the serve, so it will have diagonal spin.

Spin serves feature a lot of net clearance as their trajectories start out going up more than down. While gravity affects every serve you hit, spin augments gravity so balls will head down faster.

In contrast to a flat serve, your racquet makes a glancing blow at the ball when hitting a spin serve and for that reason, it is important that you maintain racquet head speed. Spin serves do not work if you swing easy, and that leads to perhaps the most important contribution that a spin serve can make to your game:

It helps you avoid choking.

Let's create a scenario. You, a solid 3.5 player, are serving at 15-30 and you have unloaded on a big first serve that is just an inch wide. Too bad, you think to yourself, because your opponent was nowhere near it and you would have leveled the score at 30-30. You like your first serve—you are comfortable hitting it flat, hard, and down into the court. Knowing that you have a second serve as backup, you normally lean into your first and really power through it. In practice, all you do is hit flat serves (slices are for wimps), and your percentage is nearly 50%, which is pretty good.

But now you face a second serve and the commissioners of tennis have not yet authorized a third serve. This one has to go in or you're facing 15-40. Do you hit another flat serve? At 50%, the odds are with you that you won't miss two in a row, right? Well, no—the balls have no memory. And the stakes are much higher, so it's pretty clear that you won't be hitting that serve as you normally would. But you'll still be hitting it flat, because that's all you know. You just won't swing as hard. Okay, how exactly do you do that? Do you take less backswing? Less followthrough? Slower overall swing velocity? Do you have physical checkpoints to help you make these adjustments?

In the history of tennis, you couldn't possibly find worse things to focus on when faced with a pressure situation. You will not be confident with any of those adjustments, so you will inevitably hit a creampuff serve that will resemble a delivery in a slow-pitch softball game.

In tight situations, nerves can make you tentative as you fear mistakes more than you relish opportunities. When players succumb to nerves, volleys become chops, forehands become stabs, and serves become little patty-cake swings. Spin becomes your best friend in those situations because it allows you (requires you) to take full swings at the ball. Instead of hitting directly behind the ball, your racquet brushes along its side. Instead of hitting down into the court, you hit up, providing a lot of net clearance.

Your serve percentage does not fall off when you accelerate through a spin serve; it actually rises. And you won't feel your nerves nearly as much when executing a full swing.

Is the slice serve the most important quality of a serve? No, but it might be the most important quality of a *second* serve.

Going for the gusto

And finally, we get to pace, the quality of a serve that I consider to be the least important in doubles. I don't mean to be so dismissive of it, and you could certainly make the case that this is just sour grapes dripping down these pages. I have nothing resembling a 120mph serve and it is not uncommon for me to play three full sets and record zero aces. But I will stick to my guns that having big guns is overrated. I'm also a pragmatist: few women rely on big serves in amateur tennis, so half of my audience will be sitting on the sidelines for this part of the conversation.

While I can't speak to the joy one might feel in laying into a thick first serve with regularity, I can speak with complete authority on how it feels to dismantle an opponent with a big serve. I've done that plenty of times and few things are more satisfying. The expression "live by the ace, die by the ace," is quite apt here, as many big servers develop such a reliance on their singular weapon that their games become a bit lopsided. If their serve is off, they have little else to fall back on, and that is not a comfortable feeling in the middle of a match. One or two good returns and they could be done for the day.

It's not just that I lack a natural affinity (and musculature) for the flat serve. It simply does not suit my style of play:

- The best flat servers will connect on about 50-60% of first serves. I expect to serve first serves at over 70%.

- Returns of flat serves come back much harder and faster, reducing my reaction time.

- Returns of flat serves come back much sooner, preventing me from getting into my preferred volleying position.

Everything points to my not relying on flat serves, and so I don't. And my opponents know it. Even if they have never played against me, by the middle of the second set, they have pretty much sized me up as someone who is not going to be hitting beamers up the middle.

And that's why my flat serves can be surprisingly effective. I might only hit one per match, but if I connect on it, the shock waves might reverberate for the rest of the set.

This normally plays out for me as a tight set is nearing its climax. If I'm serving at, say, 4-4, and in my third or fourth ad-in, opponents in the ad court have already seen me swing them wide about a dozen times and know that the serves I hit middle are kick serves that can be caught up to. So by now they are cheating out wide to protect their backhands a bit. The middle is wide open and if I can cheat toward the T just a bit, I could find that opening. More important, I don't need to crush the serve to win the point; just about any serve that doesn't kick up is going to be unreturnable at this point in the match. I'm not saying that it's easy for me to do; just that it is worth trying.

I often utilize an innocent ploy to facilitate this. From my normal serving position on the baseline (closer to the alley than the T), I will intentionally send an errant toss over my head, let it bounce, say sorry, and then resume. But I will have retrieved my bad toss a good two feet closer to the T, which would be my preferred position to attempt the flat serve middle. If I were to simply walk to that position at the outset of the point, opponents would likely notice. But a bad toss…who cares? I can see it now, once this book is out, any time I make a bad toss and let it drop, my opponents will move toward the middle…

Must you be nine feet tall to serve flat?

From the 1970s came this wonderful bit of tennis lore that a person would have to be over nine feet tall in order to truly hit down on a serve. The calculations involved an impressive shtick of trigonometry and captured the imagination of many, including Vic Braden who shared it with a national tennis audience (yes, during one of those rain delays).

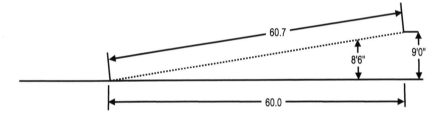

This lovely story left out two small factors: a player's reach and the law of gravity. Oh, that.

Because we cannot account for the variables of a player's wingspan or the propensity to jump into the air during the serve, more responsible calculations are just conjecture. But the general consensus is that 6' 10" Ivo Karlovic might be the only one who can literally hit a serve down into the court. The rest of us must hit up on the ball in order to navigate the net and the service box. Another reason to forego flat serves…

15

Aye Aye to I

One of the biggest surprises to me is how underutilized and underappreciated use of I-formation is at all but the highest levels of the game. This baffles me for several reasons, not the least of which is because it is not that complicated and with a bit of practice and repetition becomes quite simple. And yet, my queries in 8.0 doubles or with 3.5 and 4.0 players are usually met with "I've never tried it—how does it work?"

My hope for you is that you develop a comfort and familiarity with the I-formation. I'd like to see you come to regard it as just another strategic choice, like whether to lob or drive.

I-Formation 1A

I-formation sees both server and partner playing from the middle of the court. If you were to draw a line from one player to the other, it would create the letter I right down the middle of the court—hence its name. The core of the formation is as simple as that: both players starting in the middle of the court. From that simple definition, you can imagine why I like it so much, because I think taking control of the middle of the court is the holy grail of doubles, and here both players are starting there. In the following diagram, the server's partner is just a bit off to the side and that is a concession of age.

If you watch the pros play I, the net person is right at the net strap, crouched below the height of the net. As soon as the serve passes the net, the net person springs up. That is very much a young person's move—for us aging adult amateurs, it's easier to start just barely outside of the serving window where we don't have to crouch down.

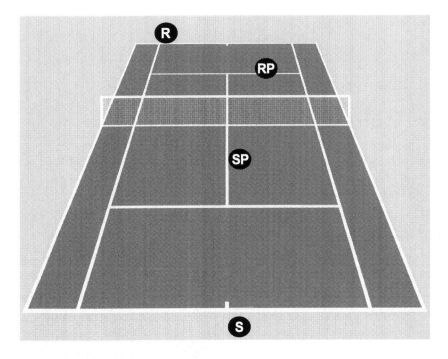

Playing I to a T
At its core, I-formation sees both players on the serving team starting in the middle of the court. One or both players will move once the ball is in play.

Let's first dispense with the popular misconception that I-formation and the so-called "Australian formation" are the same; they are not. In Australian formation, the net player does not play in the middle, but instead is located all the way over in the other service box. So imagine in the diagram above, the server's partner locates to the right to be in the middle of that service box. The presumption is that the returner has a very strong crosscourt return, so the net person is positioned to discourage the returner from hitting it. Australian is a defensive and mostly passive strategy that is not used very often. Whatever defensive measure you might want to employ can be addressed from the I without your team having to concede that much court. So I don't like Australian, I no longer play it, and I suggest you not risk the confusion of trying to consider both formations. It's much simpler to limit your options to either playing a conventional formation or playing I-formation.

Lots of movement

I-formation involves lots of movement and that alone could be unsettling for your opponents. You both start in the middle of the court, but you both can't stay there, as you have court coverage responsibilities. So one or both of you will be on the move as soon as the serve passes the net.

The decision to go I is usually in response to an opponent's strength. There are other reasons to play I that are not a reaction to the opposition, but that is a perfectly fine reason to adopt it as you begin to grow accustomed to it. In the diagram at left, for instance, let's say that your opponent in the deuce court has a strong forehand return that has been dipping at your feet as you advance to the net or has been hit for outright winners. Moving into I-formation places your partner right where those forehands would go, and by moving close to the middle, you increase the chance of steering your serve away from the forehand to begin with.

If your partner is going to stay put, then you have some work to do as there is an entire half of court for you to cover to your left. And if your right-handed backhand is not up to the task, this could be troublesome. If you choose to advance straight in to net or cover the right half of the court from the baseline, then it is your partner at the net who must move left quickly. But not too quickly: the occupational hazard of I is moving before the serve crosses the net and getting tagged by it.

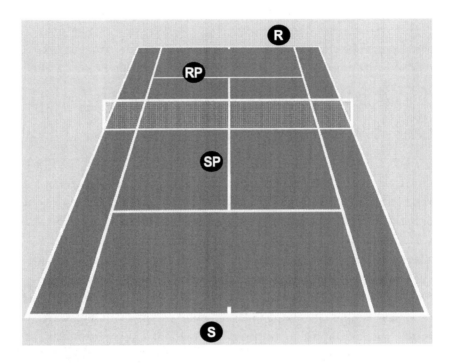

Ad Court I

Right-handers might find it easier playing I-formation in the ad court, where court coverage takes them to their forehand sides.

Moving directly across the court and then having to hit a backhand stroke or volley is not an entirely comfortable move, and for this reason right-handers might find it easier to play I in the ad court, where as you can see in this diagram, court coverage takes you to your forehand side.

Once again, some of the most potent moves can be made by righty-lefty partnerships in the deuce court, where a serve to the T might produce a weak backhand response that a left-handed volleyer can devour.

Lots of talk

Under conventional formation, you might like to signal or you might prefer not to, but in I-formation, all good teams confer or signal, usually on every point. Each of you must move in concert on a level well above conventional formation and that often changes on a point-by-point basis.

If you detect a weak backhand among your opponents, that might be all the communication needed: "I'm serving backhand." If that weak backhand is in the deuce court, your net partner doesn't have to commit to going one direction or the other but can instead simply follow the ball, with you reacting in kind. I like this approach because it promotes recognition and spontaneity, two great doubles qualities.

The real value of I-formation

If all of this talk of formation and movement is straining your brain, then let me offer an altogether different reason to play I-formation: you become a better server. If you're like most doubles players, you are always serving from a point along the baseline about 10 feet from the T, and it's been so long since you've played singles, you don't even remember what it feels like to serve from the T.

I want you to rekindle that relationship for the simple reason that most people serve better from the middle of the court. The net is lower in the middle, the angles are friendlier, and you are closer to the service box.

If you are struggling to hold or an opponent is picking on your serve, you don't need any more reason than that to try I. Move your partner over, head to the T and just serve. I'll bet you lunch that your serve will be more effective for that reason alone.

I-formation is easy to practice. Serve an entire game employing it. Maybe an entire set. Discover in which directions you and your partner are most comfortable moving and from which side it seems to work better. Your quest is to reach a sufficient comfort level so that, at 4-4 in the first set of a real match, if your partner says "let's play I," your response can be as simple as "Okay, which way do you want to go?"

16

Your First Serve Attitude Adjustment

If you are like most players, you hit your first serve really hard because you know that you have a second serve to fall back on if you miss. Unless you average better than one service winner per game, I want you to consider a cognitive shift. As intoxicating as aces and unreturnable serves are, there is a more important quality of a first serve—namely that it goes in.

Players who connect on close to 70% of their first serves tend to be among the most effective at all levels of the amateur game. *This is almost without regard for the quality of the serve.* It's not just that it creates lower stress for you not having to face down all those second serves and it's not just that hitting fewer serves is easier on your body. I also want you to consider two other factors:

- It is draining for your opponents to encounter one first serve after another. They look to put pressure on your second serve and when they can't, it becomes dispiriting.

- Opponents hope that you will feel the pressure of second serves yourself. When you don't, it is discouraging.

Accurate first serves create better second serves

When you go lights out on your first serve, the difference between it and your second serve is vast, and that is not such a good thing. By comparison, your second serve becomes more attackable and more vulnerable. This also requires that you practice two starkly different motions, and that is not the cleanest recipe for success, either.

But when you hit first serves at 80% intensity, you are grooving a motion that is more similar to your second serve. By narrowing the gap between first and second serve, you reduce the stress associated with hitting second serves. After feeling drained from all those first serves you hit, imagine how opponents must feel when they finally get a second serve and it doesn't look much different.

This is all easy for me to say—I top out well below 100mph on serves. If I actually were capable of hitting big serves, would I be singing a different tune? Perhaps. But I would also know the frustration of being dependent on a move that requires a high degree of precision, and I would experience the angst of never knowing for sure whether it will show up until I begin play.

Those who hit serves at 80% intensity and with a lot of net clearance can derive confidence from knowing that they don't need their serves to be totally on in order to play well, and they can take comfort in knowing that if their serves are off, it is easier to fix them.

17

The Riddle of
The Return

There is a reason why this section of the book features four chapters on serve and only one on return, and it isn't because returning serve is unimportant. In fact, it might be the most important part of the game.

Unlike other aspects of the game, creating more awareness of the return won't necessarily make you better at it. In fact, it might make you worse. It's kind of like the NBA's great shooters who go cold from the free throw line. What do you say to them? Most coaches agree to just leave them alone and try to keep them from stewing over it.

But you didn't buy this book so I could advise you to "let it happen." Here are a few ideas that have a bit more meat on their bones than that.

Just get the &#$@% thing back

You probably also didn't buy this book to read that the secret to returning the serve is to return the serve. Wow, stop the presses. But hear me out, because all too often when facing a really good server, we defenders try to hit the perfect return. I fall victim to that all the time: he's serving lights out and

I'm still trying to crack winners up the middle of the court. Why am I sensible elsewhere on the court and yet so dumb with my returns?

The heading for this section is more of a suggested mind-set than a tactical recommendation. When you should consider yourself lucky to just get the ball back, please just try to get the ball back! Several potentially good things happen when you do that:

- You get better at handling big serves and don't fear them as much.

- You frustrate your opponent who was expecting a service winner.

- You don't have time to think so you don't. Thinking is overrated.

- And every so often, you will meet a ball cleanly and return all of that pace back to the sender. That will likely be one of the best feelings you can have on the court.

Watch the &#$@% ball

The No. 1 tennis fundamental might be violated more often on the return than on every other stroke combined. It's easy to understand why: everything happens so quickly, you often never see the ball in the first place. And the further north of age 40 you travel, the more often that seems to happen.

But even if you don't pick the ball up as well as you used to, you must pretend that you do. When you take your eye off the ball, you tend to lift your head, which lifts your shoulders, which messes with your swing plane, which results in legendary frame jobs.

On the other hand, a quiet head gives you a fighting chance. It promotes a simple swing and increases your margin for error. You might not actually be able to watch the ball all the way into your racquet, but acting as if you can is good enough.

Look for &#$@% clues

Have you heard the story about how Andre Agassi seized the upper hand against Boris Becker for the better part of five years? Becker was famous for serving with his tongue out, and according to Agassi, he observed that Becker would reveal his intention on serve based on where

Out front

Ana Ivanovic has sent her toss about two feet into the court. From that position she will be hitting a flat or slice serve.

his tongue flapped: To the right side of his mouth, he would serve right; to the left side, he would serve left.

I wouldn't be able to detect that my opponent was serving with his mouth open, let alone that his tongue was out, let alone where said tongue was located. Who even looks at the server's mouth in the first place? This would be utterly implausible if it were not for the fact that Agassi might have been the best returner in history and one of the reasons for that was his 20-15 eyesight.

We mere mortals should focus on more visible signs, like the location of your opponent's toss and the position of your opponent's back. Those two factors can tell you a lot, across both genders (and the following section uses pronouns interchangeably).

Toss out in front?

If your opponent's toss is more than two feet into the court, odds are that he is either serving flat or with a hard slice. A good server can go middle (flat) or wide (slice) from that toss in the deuce court, but will not be able to serve wide as easily in the ad court.

When I see a right-hander tossing out in front in the ad court, I look middle and might even cheat that way by a step. In the deuce court, I need the additional cue of the placement of the toss. If it is directly in front, I suspect that she is serving middle. If the toss is a bit more to her right (or to her left from my vantage point), I anticipate that she might carve around the side of the ball and take me wide.

Better servers can carve the ball or hit it flat from the same toss, in which case your best course of action is to take a step inside the baseline and try to meet the ball early. This is challenging, I know, as you are taking your own time away, but you can't cover middle and wide serves from a foot behind the baseline; the wide serve will slide away from you.

Standing in might seem scary at first, but it is a skill worth cultivating. It will improve your reaction time, teach you to abbreviate your backswing, and encourage a no-thought response to serves. All the great returners in the professional game step in to hit their returns. It might be one of the more valuable additions you can make to your stroke collection.

Toss over the head?

Servers who do not toss the ball into the court might be harder to read but chances are they are not going to drop the boom on you. From a ball position more directly over his head, the server will likely impart some type of spin on the ball and that will reduce the serve's raw velocity.

Over the head

While you can't see the toss, the arch of Roger Federer's back makes it clear that he has tossed the ball straight up and is about to explode up to the ball and impart topspin on it.

That might not make it any easier, though, as good servers can load the ball up from that toss, hit it deep, and place it.

The secondary clue is his back: Is he going at the ball with a straight lower back or is he arching it as he tosses? The arched back is the telltale sign of a server who is about to kick a serve—usually up the middle in the deuce court and out wide in the ad court. Off of a right-hander's racquet, that ball is going to bounce high and to the right (see the diagram on page 86).

While you might have time to catch up to it, the high bounce could be troublesome, especially if it is to your one-handed backhand. If you allow the ball to reach waist level, it might be at shoulder level before you know it. And if you wait for the ball to reach its apex (as you can often do with a normal serve), you might be so far off the court by then that you'll feel like you're in jail.

Once again, the move to make is to meet it early, before it kicks up into your eyes and/or takes you off the court. Against severe kick serves, I will literally half-volley returns. I don't care how difficult it might be to time the stroke; I'd choose that poison over the serve that would otherwise bounce above my shoulders.

The alternate response to these types of serves is to lob. If you go that route, then you want to do the opposite: you want to wait for the ball to do its thing. It's hard enough to take a full swing on a ball met on the rise; lobbing off of that shot is nearly impossible. With your racquet face open, a kicking serve might really spring off of your strings—long, wide, or maybe both—so you will need to adjust for that.

Turn your &#$@% mind off

The underlying concept to these tactics is that you learn to react to what you see, without conscious thought. That won't happen at first and that's okay. As you first start watching for these clues, not only should you use your conscious mind, you should do so emphatically. Say it out loud as the toss is going up, report to yourself on what type of serve it was and what the toss and body position looked like. Prepare a complete briefing for yourself on what you observed and what type of serve you encountered.

I'm not advising you to be a jerk about it, and I certainly don't advocate your identifying serves in mid-flight during matches. These are exercises best done with—how did we say it to our kids?—with your inside voice and only in practice matches. But the theory is sound: using all of your senses to identify and observe service motions is the best way to cultivate automatic responses to them.

Take the fault test

Have you noticed that some of your best returns come on serves that are long? If you're like most people, when you see that the serve is out, you immediately relax your muscles, you loosen up your swing, you quiet your head and shoulders, and you follow through to an easy finish.

Aren't these all of the things that you should do against serves that are in? How come you don't do them? Why do you reserve your best return form for serves that don't count? Doesn't that infuriate you??

These are not rhetorical questions—you need to ask them of yourself. There is a much improved return of serve waiting for the person who is able to answer them.

The next time you pure a backhand return on a serve three inches long, ask yourself about it. You only have about five seconds to have this private conversation, so try to tune right in. What did you do right, what did it feel like? How did your body feel? What can you transfer to your for-real return?

I'm not trying to send you to a shrink and you don't have to be one to understand that there is nothing at stake on the return of a missed serve. That is the simplest answer for why we relax: there is nothing to lose. When a point is on the line, you are more deliberate and careful. But do those two behaviors translate into a better stroke? Usually not.

Whenever I drill a return on a fault, I notice that I don't pop up at all. My head stays really level and I don't get the yips that often invade my real returns. That's definitely something that I can bring to my real returns and it has provided me with a mantra for crucial returns: head down...head down...head down.

Study the way you return missed serves and see if you can create your own mantra from it.

Returning second serves

Finally, we move to the most maddening aspect of the return game: the inevitable fact that we often do worse against second serves than we do against first serves. I don't want to overstate this problem—if it were that commonplace, it would negate all of my advice about getting your first serve in—but it does seem that the serves that often trouble people the most are the break point pattycakers that are inexplicably returned into the middle of the net.

If you suffer from this malady, it is likely that you respond to these half-swing second serves with a half swing of your own. When encountering a ball that has no pace, the worst thing you can do is make a swing that also has no pace. Against a no-pace serve, you need to compensate with a long, full swing. You don't need to swing hard or wild and you don't need to rush yourself. Take your time, perhaps more time than you would normally take. But when you get to the ball, don't cheat the swing: take it all the way back and finish nice and high.

◆

Have you detected the recurrent theme of this chapter? The more you can go brain-dead, the better you will return. Your body knows how to execute a proper return; your mission is to allow your body to do it, without interference from an overactive mind. You need to keep your conscious mind from getting in the way and that's not so easy because it wants to play, too. So you need to resort to deceit and trickery to make it believe that its services are not needed. Anything you can do to promote reactive, instinctual, and mindless tennis will help you hit better returns and play better doubles.

Can it really be that simple? Well, if it were, we'd all quit the game out of boredom. But it should be our continual quest to try to make it that easy.

Going Mental

One of the joys of writing this book has been the discoveries I have made along the way. With almost every chapter, I have had a general sense of what to write about, and then upon going deeper, I have uncovered a treasure of digressions, sidetracks, and plot twists. And I have indulged most of them, much to my delight and, I hope, to your enjoyment.

All of that goes double for this group of chapters. These are all topics I have thought about for decades and discussed over post-match beers on many occasions. But putting them into words? That's a whole different thing.

The topics in this book were not written so that you would agree with all of them, but rather, to make you think, scrutinize, perhaps dispute, and ultimately reach your own conclusions. That goes triple for this section. I hope you enjoy the ride.

18

Warmup: Psych Out Or Psych Up?

Let's start with the obvious: In the five-minute warmup allowed in USTA matches and other forms of competition, there is virtually nothing that you can do to physically prepare yourself to play at your best. Hitting for five minutes? Ground strokes, volleys, overheads, *and* serves? Please. Your real warmup needs to have already happened. The pros take an hour to properly prepare; you should take at least 15 minutes.

The whole notion of the warmup is a bit bizarre when you think about it. I play five sports competitively, and in none of the other ones do I warm up with my opponents. In fact, I can think of no other sport on the planet that does that. (Racquetball, maybe? Perhaps badminton?) No, those first five minutes after you step on to the court with your opponents is a phenomenon onto itself. Here are a few thoughts on how you can make the most of this unusual custom.

The assumption for this chapter is that you are playing a match of some consequence and that you have already warmed up with your doubles partner or with other members of your team before encountering your opponents. So this won't apply to Tuesday night doubles with your buddies where you show up, stretch, warm up, and play.

Give nothing, take everything

If you think your objective for the five-minute warmup is to prepare your strokes for battle, let me suggest an attitude adjustment. Your objective for the warmup is to glean everything you can about your opponents while at the same time revealing nothing about yourself. Do you have a huge forehand? You've already hit 30 of them in your real warmup, so there is no need to show how huge it is now. Are you particularly quick around the court? Love hitting backhand volleys? Backpedaling to pick overheads out of the sky? Whatever strengths your game possesses, what is to be gained by showing them? Let your opponents figure them out once the match begins.

Meanwhile, you're looking for clues about what makes your opponents tick. But what if they have already read this chapter and are deliberately concealing from you their own strengths? There are a few things that most players do during warmup that could reveal their true tendencies. That is what you are looking for. For instance:

One hand or two?

Very few players with one-handed backhands are able to hit with authority balls that are above shoulder level. (This is why Rafael Nadal owns Roger Federer on clay courts.) If you see one hand on the backhand, start thinking now of high-bouncing serves and looping groundstrokes.

Frying pans?

Pay no attention to how well your opponents volley during warmup; focus only on how they hit them. Do they use the same western grip for forehand volleys that they do for groundstrokes? If so, that is a stroke that is likely to betray them when they start to feel pressure. At critical junctures of a match, you might not need to go for winners; it might be enough to make them hit just one more volley with that fragile grip.

Same thing with overheads. Do they turn their shoulders and get perpendicular to your lob or do they hit that with a frying pan grip, as well?

Scraping the surface

How do your opponents handle balls at their feet? This one is not intuitive, but I find that the ones who meticulously bend their knees and hit perfect low and half-volleys are the ones most likely to break down.

How many perfect low volleys can we aging amateurs hit in one match? At some point, our joints are going to mutiny and then so will that stroke.

The players who worry me are the ones who offer up only a shallow knee bend and an almost nonchalant wave of the racquet for a half-volley. Without meaning to, they are telling me that they have hit a million of those shots, they don't fear them, and more important, they know how to hit them with minimal amount of joint stress.

Scouting the serve

Sorry, I have no insight for you here. I have been burned so many times by incorrect conclusions on opposing service motions that I no longer allow myself to draw any. More times than I can count, I have been fooled by horrific looking serves in warmup that proved to be unbreakable in the match.

The only thing I do take stock in during service warmup is the height of the toss, especially on windy days. As for the direction of the toss, I'll refer you back one chapter to a set of recognition skills that you can develop to help you become a better returner.

Who's intimidating whom?

Implicit in my advice across this chapter is the conclusion that I place little value in the prospect of psyching out my opponents. Your mileage may vary here, and if we meet in a match, I hope you try to intimidate me by showing off the most incredibly awesome parts of your game. I'm certainly intimidatable, just like every other human on the planet, but nothing you do in those five minutes of warmup can accomplish that. Doing it across the two hours of the match might get the job done.

The strongest part of my game is my movement at the net and you will never see me show that to you during warmup. Assuming I am properly stretched out already, I will stretch for zero shots at the net during warmup and will hit as few volley winners as possible. Our match will start with you having no clue as to my ability to move at the net.

It's probably arrogant in the first place to think that I could send any message to my opponents during warmup, but if I were able to, I would be hoping to send the opposite of intimidation. The thought that I would want my opponent to have is this: "This guy doesn't look that good. This might be an easy two sets."

In other words, I want to show my opponents so little of my game that they conclude that I have no game. That means hitting every groundstroke right back to them, every volley into the middle of the court, only medium-speed and medium-depth shots while they are at the net. And I will run for nothing—every shot hit away from me is a winner.

I want the warmup to suggest that this is about to be the greatest mismatch in history!

The one exception is overhead. I snap off overheads at pretty sharp angles and with severe pronation, and the older I get, the less able I am to hit those without loosening up my shoulder. I'll hit them in my "real" warmup, of course, but in order to hit that shot, my shoulder wants as much lubrication as I can give it. That is the one stroke that I am truly warming up during warmup. Everything else is discovery and obfuscation.

Is this tactic for you? Only you can answer that. There is certainly something to be said for gaining confidence from the feeling that your game is superior to your opponents and that you have made them aware of that. It's not as if I begin the match brimming with confidence when my sole focus is to create the exact opposite impression. This is just one of the many games within the game; one of the countless moves on the chess board that hovers just above the court.

It happened on court

Because I stop short of warming up right-handed, I am unable to keep under wraps one of the most prominent aspects of my game. But I recently encountered an opponent who did almost that. After hitting every backhand with one hand in warmup—strokes and returns— he went into the ad court in our mixed doubles match, stepped in on a high-bouncing serve I kicked into his corner, and promptly whistled a two-hander into my alley.

It was one of at least two dozen winners that he hit from his two-handed backhand in a straight-set victory over us. When I asked him about it afterward, he acknowledged its value as a decoy. "That's not why I do it, though. Ever since shoulder surgery, I have found that the best way to get my shoulder ready for the torque is to hit with one hand. It forces me to rotate more and to prepare earlier. And hey, if it messes with your head a little bit, that's not the worst thing."

♦

We will continue this convo in the next chapter, as that topic directly relates to this one.

19

Is it Possible to Know too Much?

Bless the hearts of my women captains on mixed doubles teams—they are so incredibly well prepared, usually the product of exhaustive research of results and methodical note-taking during and after matches. (If this sounds like gender discrimination, well, it is. I've never known men to do that; we lack both the patience and dedication.)

Before a match, I might get the following briefing from my captain: "Rick, your opponents played a lot at No. 2 last season. He doesn't have a huge serve but he places it well. Not a lot of movement but he anticipates well. She is quick and likes to volley; don't be surprised if she poaches against both of you."

I am tremendously grateful for the good intentions here, but I would rather not be that well informed and I know that I'm not alone in that sentiment. There are three reasons why you might not want to receive a full scouting report on your opponents:

You become overconfident

If you receive a favorable report, it creates false confidence, as if you can now phone in your victory. Confidence is a wonderful commodity that can inspire you to play your best. Confidence might be the best feeling to have before a match. And if that is the best feeling, perhaps the worst thing you can do before a match is to harbor the feeling that you are entitled to a win. That could turn you into a basket case.

You become underconfident

A close second is the feeling of impending doom that often comes with information about how good your opponents are. It is almost impossible for you to listen to a positive appraisal of your opponents and *not* conclude that they will own you. No matter how tempered your captain's words are, you are going to hear in your head that your opponents belong on the tour.

Results in tennis are too dependent upon playing styles to place stock in either of these scouting reports. And captains are only human, too—they are going to see those opponents through the prism of their own playing styles. So you have one biased human putting words into your biased and flawed brain about what you should expect from a pair of equally-flawed humans playing a game that is the master of all of us. Too many variables!

You cheat the learning process

Perhaps the most important reason to not be too informed of your opposition is what that information does to your own quest for knowledge. In short, it can derail it. If someone tells you everything that you presumably need to know, then why bother figuring it out for yourself? Why not save that mental energy for other issues that will invariably arise during a match?

That is a troublesome conclusion.

As I have noted in several chapters, one of the most important skills you can employ in good doubles is detective work: figuring out a good path to playing your best, determining appropriate strategies, and ferreting out the strengths and weaknesses of your opponents. Who has the better return and off of which wing, forehand or backhand? How well do they backpedal off the net? How easily do they get down for half-volleys? And which do they prefer, low or high volleys? These types of discoveries are best made from an empty canvas, and being given too much information ahead of time could short-circuit the process.

There are two other factors that could make excess scouting and advance information a dubious proposition:

- The scout might have watched the team in a completely different circumstance that might have no bearing on the match that you are about to play against the same team. "They have excellent hands at the net," I once heard regarding a team we were about to play. That was based on a match against two players who hit hard flat returns against them and they hit waist-high volleys all day long. We were more of a chip-and-charge team and the softer balls that they had to field at their ankles produced an entirely different dynamic.

- The only thing that matters is what our opponents do today, not what they did a month ago. They hit every overhead in sight last month; does that mean they will do that today? Should we decide never to lob in response to that? We're all amateurs, unable to play with the type of consistency that the pros show. They need to prove that they can do those amazing things today.

Finally, I place no stock in the notion that knowing things ahead of time allows you to save mental energy. Mental energy should not be treated like a precious resource. I'd rather you think of it as a candle: once you light one, it is easier to light others, and you do not surrender any of the first flame when you create other flames. Focus begets focus and lack of focus creates vacuums.

The challenge to all of this is reconciling the concepts here with the general advice I have offered several times that you play your best when you turn off your mind. How can you develop mental energy and go brain-dead at the same time? This sounds like quite the contradiction.

I will leave the more articulate discussions on this topic to the professional sports psychologists (google "sports psychology" and tennis to read lots of articles on this). Suffice it to say that the brain is an amazing component to human performance. It is able to process information while at the same time rely on instinct. This is the sign of a player who is in the zone: she is able to react to external events she observes and still call upon her instincts. Good competitors can problem-solve and turn off their brains at the same time. They can play with both intensity and calm.

In the next chapter, we come back down to Earth…

20

The Value of Being Boring

This chapter will be the antithesis of the one that someone else will write on the value of keeping opponents guessing. Not that there is anything wrong with that strategy—if your opponents are constantly wondering what you are going to do next, they are not concentrating on their own games. That makes it a perfectly legitimate approach to take to a match.

It's just not particularly noteworthy. I'd rather write about the opposite: how effective and even devastating it can be to be predictable. Winning through boredom is fascinating.

Let's say that you have found something that works in a match. Let's say that it is a serve up the middle of the ad court that slices away from your opponent and instead of getting around the ball to drive (take your pick here, his or her) forehand, she tends to slide under the ball. Her return alternates between sailing long, floating wide, or sitting up so you or your partner can put away a volley.

You're not really sure if her backhand is better and at some point you figure that you'll have to keep her honest and hit a few serves out wide. In fact, she is now daring you to do just that by standing a foot closer to the middle of the court.

So what do you do? However tempting it might be, the smart money is on changing nothing. Keep hitting those serves down the middle until she can prove to you that she can handle it. And what constitutes handling it? One point won off of a good forehand return? Two? Keep going…

Reminiscent of the mixed doubles match Elaine and I played against the guy who couldn't hit a backhand return (see Chapter 8), there is no compelling reason whatsoever for you to change anything. Be boring; be predictable. Keep serving middle.

Granted, if you choose to serve wide and you blast an ace, well, that's pretty good. I concede that doing that would be pretty darn effective. Then you tell your opponent that you own her on both sides of the service box.

But the odds are not with you and just about anything else will feel like a bit of a concession. You did it either in response to her change in positioning or you did it because you just didn't feel like serving middle any longer.

But continuing to serve middle sends the following message: "You haven't caught up to one of these yet and I'm going to give you plenty of chances to. When you finally do, we'll tally up the score—it will be something like 1 out of 10—and then we'll just start over. In fact, here comes another one right now…oh darn, you missed."

If you surprise your opponent with an unexpected serve, that could become part of the explanation as to why she missed it. But when you remove the element of surprise from the situation—when you all but tell her out loud that you're doing it again—and she still loses the point to you, the conclusion is inescapable: "There is nothing you can do so you might as well just give up now."

Creating sameness on the court also creates incredible tension for your opponents because they know that eventually you are going to change it up. The longer you go, the greater that tension.

This plays out for me as a little drama in the deuce court. I prefer to hit my left-handed slice down the middle, where it usually goes to a backhand and it affords us an opportunity to take control of the middle of the court. I know how to hit a kick serve out wide on that side, too, but I prefer serving middle.

I often keep score to myself just how far into the match I can go before I serve wide. If I am holding consistently, I won't serve wide at all. If I don't have to face any 0-30 points, I will continue to serve middle. If I can make it through the entire first set only serving middle in the deuce court, I consider that to be a private victory. I have sent the message to my opponent in the deuce court that I can prevail over him or her while only using half the court, and I set up the wide serve as a looming threat.

Once many years ago, I went all the way to 5-5 in a second-set tiebreaker without serving wide once. At 5-5 in the breaker, I concluded that it was the right time and it so surprised my opponent that he made no play on the ball at all, even though it landed at least a foot from either line. He was pretty much toast at that point and we made sure to steer the first ball we could to him on the 6-5 match point, which he netted.

Winning while being predictable is one of the most psychologically devastating things you can do.

Another viewpoint

Playing editor Marilyn Morrell-Kristal has been competing in doubles her entire adult life and has adopted a different philosophy, based on candy.

Yes, it's important to continue to exploit the weaker service return side of your opponent, but after a while, I will choose to offer to my opponents the shot that they most like to hit. I refer to this as a "piece of candy."

Most of the time, they are so eager and thrilled to have their favorite shot, that they overreact, making big errors. Of course, the risk is always there that they can hit a winner, but I take that risk because I don't want them to get too comfortable or grooved on what I deem is the weaker side. I wouldn't want them to gain unnecessary confidence in their weaker stroke. So a little bit of candy every so often can go a long way.

Momentum and Risk

A first cousin to the topic of the previous chapter is the question of seizing and maintaining momentum and measuring risk. These topics really find their feet in the sport of golf, where one bad swing can literally ruin an otherwise good round. Can that happen in tennis? When is the right time to attempt a risky shot? And what constitutes momentum in a sport as fluid as ours?

This is a difficult question to address because history is full of conflict. Watch how I paint two entirely different pictures from one famous match.

The year is 1980 and John McEnroe and Bjorn Borg are meeting in the Wimbledon final. McEnroe was looking for his first Wimbledon title, having beaten Jimmy Connors in the semis. He enters a fourth-set tiebreaker down two sets to one. Statistically speaking, the fourth set is practically dead even, and the tiebreak proceeds well into overtime. McEnroe survives numerous match points and subsists in a perennial state of being two points from defeat for nearly 20 minutes. While not exactly known for being risk averse, McEnroe nonetheless enters a sustained period of play in which he literally misses no volleys. Borg would have to pass him outright to win points (which he did with regularity) because every ball that finds McEnroe's strings also finds the court.

McEnroe wins that tiebreaker 18-16, a duel that would be replayed for years and decades during rain delays at the All-England Club. (Today's roof over Centre Court might be wonderful, but it will also preclude today's younger players from watching this classic battle the way we got to.)

On the strength of that low-risk strategy ("I just said to myself that I'm not going to miss a single volley"), McEnroe enters the fifth set brimming with confidence and full of momentum. Furthermore, he creates numerous early opportunities to seize control of the final set, having reached break point in two of Borg's first three service games and 0-30 in the other. But Borg rebuffs him with an entirely different strategy. The player who once described his typical strategy in the most risk-free way ("I try to hit the ball deep and down the middle—that seems to work well for me."), Throws caution to the wind in that fifth set and on multiple occasions hits second-serve aces to overturn break points or climb out of 0-30 and 15-30 holes.

McEnroe's victory in the fourth-set tiebreaker garners most of the reminiscence these days, but Borg's heroics in the fifth set might have been more impressive. A visibly frustrated McEnroe (surprise) loses the momentum, and ultimately, the match.

Which moral of the story is more apt: how McEnroe seized momentum by playing high-percentage tennis to win that famous tiebreak or how Borg recaptured the momentum by assuming all that risk?

Golfers refer to this as the risk-reward ratio: is the risk worth the reward? In that sport, it is pretty easy to measure, as carrying that four iron 175 yards over a lake might get you on the green, while not hitting it just right will get you a triple bogey. But in tennis, the ratio is not quite as well defined, especially in the amateur ranks. Put yourself in Borg's position—you are serving at 4-4, 40-30, and you miss your first serve. Is that the time to load up on a second, as he did? If you miss it, you are back at deuce, which is not the end of the world. But if you are fortunate enough to connect on that serve, you are rewarded with a game.

Now change the scenario: the score is 30-40, not 40-30, and you stand ready to hit a second serve. The reward for connecting on that risky serve is a measly deuce and if you miss, you're broken. That ratio is not as easy to justify, is it? (Wouldn't it be something if tennis incorporated a level-of-difficulty factor, as do many Olympic sports? If you hit a second-serve ace at deuce, you automatically win the game...)

When you accept risk, you need to weigh its entire cost, because it might not just be a point or a game. You might also be risking your hard-fought momentum. While some believe that the reward for having gained momentum is the right to go for risky shots, I would argue the opposite: momentum on your side should be your cue to stay the course and keep doing what earned you that momentum in the first place.

Irrespective of how you choose to respond to momentum, we also need to weigh the value of momentum in the first place. A tennis match is not a sprint, it's a marathon, and momentum inevitably changes more than once. (It astonishes me how fleeting momentum is in a five-set match on the men's tour—it might shift between players a dozen times.) Outside of a total mismatch, it is incredibly rare for a team to be able to stay in high gear throughout an entire match—just look at the statistics that show how vulnerable teams are to a service break immediately after they have broken serve themselves.

This is like the clenched fist exercise I shared in Chapter 9, it is practically impossible to start in high gear and stay there throughout an entire match. So perhaps the most important quality of good competitors across a two-hour match is not how well they perform once they have captured momentum but how they respond when they lose it. Because we all do. Do you and your partner show your frustration, play what-if, and generally show an inability to get past bad things? Or do you display an emotional maturity about the natural ebb and flow of a match and expect, plan for, and take in stride the rough patches that inevitably occur across two hours of competition?

I don't have to look far to find examples of each. In a recent 9.0 match, my partner and I were cruising. Up a break in the first set, I was serving at 30-0, and ripped a first serve up the middle that created an easy overhead opportunity. Which I hit long. So instead of 40-0 and a point away from going up 4-1, I was serving to the guy while still thinking about that opportunity lost. He guessed right on a serve I tried to jam him with, stepped in, and put a ball at my feet. Then came a ball down my partner's line, then a net cord winner, and before we had time to say "what happened??" we were changing ends on serve.

While receiving at 2-3, it was impossible for me to stay in the moment as I continued to dwell on the service game that I gave away. Normally, I can get past my choke jobs without too much collateral damage but this one just ate at me. And my poor partner had to witness all of it, not able to do much to help. (When the guy goes off the rails in mixed doubles, it can really get ugly.)

Ten minutes later, our opponents were changing ends, having broken us again to go up 4-3. Five minutes later, it was 5-3, and while we finally held serve, our opponents were about to serve for the set at 5-4 with all of the momentum on their side.

It was my partner who pulled us (me) out of the doldrums by reciting one of our regular mantras when opponents are serving for a set. "Let's make them earn it," she said. Such a simple phrase and yet such a powerful message. *Let's make them earn it* reminds us that we don't need to go for broke or play spectacular tennis. Instead, we should force our opponents to make the shots necessary to win points, and at the same time give them every opportunity to show their nerves as the stakes rise.

It centers us, it puts us back in the moment, and it suggests an easy-to-follow course of action: get balls back in play and force the other guys to earn their victory.

It worked. We chipped, we lobbed, we covered the center of the court, we didn't try to do too much with our shots, and we broke at 15 with, fittingly, a payback net cord winner.

We arrived at the sanctuary of 5-5 and the momentum had clearly shifted back our way. Now it was they who were frustrated and we who had a path to victory in the set. So what do I do? I try for too big of a volley, go for too much on a lob hit over my backhand side, attempt an ill-advised cross on a wide serve, and we give the break right back to them.

What an idiot I am! Had I learned nothing about managing momentum? Was I playing competitive tennis for the first time? Experiences like these remind us all that we are just one bad decision away from losing control of a match and that we need to continually relearn the lessons of when to play percentage tennis and when to take risks.

I refer you back to Chapter 8, When to Change Strategy, the gist of which is this: You should change your game when you are losing and you should stay the course when you are winning. That sentence could easily be rewritten: You should take risks when you are losing and you should play percentage tennis when you are winning.

In Chapter 23, I share with you how I really treat the fleeting concept of momentum. Oh yes…that's the chapter that is all about lying…

Channeling Against the Choke

"**N**ovak, if you win your quarterfinal match, you'll play either Murray or Nadal. Have you thought at all about whom you'd rather go up against?"

"I'm just trying to get through this next match. I just need to go one match at a time and focus on what I need to do against [Joe Nobody]."

This typical interview surely accounts for some of the most boring television in the history of broadcasting, played out at every single major by every single player who has ever had a microphone thrust in his or her face. Wait, there's one that's even worse:

"Maria, what do you need to do today against [Jane Nobodyova]?"

"I just need to go out there and concentrate on each point, not try to do too much, take what she gives me, and oh yes, have fun out there."

Let's start with the obvious—that no players in their right minds would reveal their strategies before a match when, in the modern age, it would arrive on an opponent's smartphone screen about 30 seconds later. But that's not the only reason why the pros are so boring—after all, they've been being boring on camera since before Al Gore invented the Internet. They know that putting blinders on best prepares them for the match ahead.

There might not be a major in your future, or a television interview, but you would be well-advised to consider the same approach, especially if you battle with nerves during competition.

The anatomy of the choke

Why do people get nervous? I face that question on a daily basis, thanks to my day job coaching people on how to speak in public. I regularly cite the Jerry Seinfeld joke about how people would rather be in the casket than delivering the eulogy. (No joke, actually: In the 2012 Book of Lists, public speaking ranks as our No. 1 fear. Death is No 7.)

At the biological level, your nerves are an anachronistic response to a perceived threat. When our prehistoric ancestors faced a mortal threat, like a tiger ready to attack, their choices were to fight or run away, and in either case, the adrenalin that their bodies produced helped them do that. This so-called fight-or-flight response no longer serves us—having our bodies flooded with adrenalin in no way helps us prepare for a challenge in which our fine motor skills are required.

It is also not terribly helpful that we humans have an easier time thinking about the past or the future than we do the present. Your body knows how to perform a certain task, but when your mind begins to focus on the last time you attempted it and failed, or worse, dwells on what happens if you fail at it again, that just gunks up everything.

Dwelling on past mistakes and worrying about mistakes we might make are practically instinctual, and they stand as two gigantic impediments to performance.

Can you avoid nerves?

Our biology and our psychology have not evolved with the times. Wouldn't it be great if our bodies were to automatically produce endorphins when the stakes rise? And wouldn't it be something if we could create a state of temporary amnesia when called upon to focus on a particular task?

No, we're stuck with nerves instead, so the question becomes how you deal with that inconvenience. Your teammates might be well-intended by assuring you that there is no reason to be nervous, but that is beyond your control. As I tell my clients about the specter of giving a public presentation, you can't make yourself not be nervous. You either are or you are not, and given those two choices, I'd rather you be nervous. And then I share with them a quote from hall-of-fame baseball player Reggie Jackson:

If I'm not nervous, then there is something wrong. If I don't feel butterflies, maybe I don't care as much as I should.

I love that quote because it gives you permission to be nervous. Your nerves are a sign that you are doing something that matters to you, something whose outcome is important to you. Also, your nerves provide energy—for all of the trouble that it might cause, adrenalin is an extremely efficient fuel.

So the first order of business is to accept the fact that you will be nervous. Don't try to ignore or eliminate your nerves; that won't work. Embrace them as part of the whole experience that you are privileged to be having.

Nervousness means that it matters to you and that is a very good thing. The question before you is how you deal with all of that excess energy. How do you channel all of that energy into positive performance?

The mind/body relationship

The first part of the challenge is easier for tennis players than it is for my clients. My clients don't get to run around on a tennis court; they are stuck in an environment in which they are just standing there. When their hearts begin to race, they have no easy recourse. One of the ways to channel nervous energy is to use large muscles instead of small ones. I tell them to make big gestures with their upper body and speak from their diaphragm instead of their throat. Focus on big muscles, not small ones.

We tennis players can use big muscles more easily, but we cannot ignore our small muscle groups. You must hit delicate volleys and deft lobs and call upon the thousands of tiny muscles in your wrists, hands, and fingers. And that is not so easy to do when every system in your body is operating faster than factory specification.

You might think at first that fast-twitch muscles would operate better if the rest of your body were moving at a fast pace, also, but that is not how it works. The small muscles in your body work best when they are encased in calm. The slower your body systems are working, the more readily fast-twitch muscles can fire. The obvious analogy is the feline—watch the cat respond to his environment and you will be witness to one of the finer athletes in our midst. A cat who is minding his own business on the top of a fence is at complete rest and calm. When he hears or sees a disturbance, he responds with only the body parts needed to better perceive its source. He turns his head and watches or listens; no other part of his body moves. If the commotion is caused by his owner taking out the trash, he puts his head back down. If the noise is the dog next door, he immediately springs to action, ready to dash in any direction.

Can you be *quick as a cat?* Yes, but it will require a level of mastery that most humans do not think about. In order to move with that type of efficiency, you must quiet the rest of your body, and if a gallon of adrenalin has just been dumped into it, that won't be so easy.

While we are jumping amid all of these analogies—from the CEO at a lecturn to the cat on a fence—let's offer up one more: the 10-year-old girl about to perform at a piano recital. Talk about your stress inducer. Talk about perceived threats and high stakes—this one is tops on the list! In addition to teaching scales and arpeggios, the piano instructor will coach her young protégé to take deep slow breaths, roll her shoulders, and maybe even close her eyes for a moment once she takes the bench. These are all mechanisms to help slow down her world.

Finally, one more analogy: the racehorse. Her handlers affix vision-blocking devices (blinders) alongside her eyes so that she won't be distracted by the other horses next to her. Her jockey wants her to be completely focused on the task at hand.

How can you slow down your world when facing break point on your serve? How can you shut out all of the distractions around you or within you? Those are the $64K questions here.

Turning back time

The cognitive leap that I am going to ask of you here is to regard these distractions not so much as a matter of what, but as a matter of *when*. Two of the most notable distractions to performance are fretting about errors that you just made and worrying about errors you might make. The past and the future are not your friends here.

We don't say to ourselves: "Oh no, I am making an error right now!"

Instead we say: "You missed that volley. You suck."

And: "What if I make another error on this next point."

Is there a mortal threat before you on the tennis court? No. Despite all perceptions to the contrary, you are not about to die out there. It is also unlikely that the result of your match will affect your career, your marriage, or your financial well-being. None of the perceived threats actually exist in the present moment—there is no tiger staring you down—they are all about things that might happen.

That is why the pros are so boring in their interviews: they know that talking about the last match or about a future match is a distraction. All they want to do is focus on the task at hand. This match. This game. This point.

And that is the very best response to nerves and pressure. It is also perhaps the most important skill you can develop as a competitor, superseding most of the advice that this book offers. And I choose my words carefully here: this is a skill. You can learn to do this.

Let's set the scene. It's the third set and you're facing match point against you, serving at 4-5, 30-40. The stakes can hardly be higher here—lose this point and you go home. The nervous, conscious mind is invariably going to some bad places here.

It's going to the past: *How could I have missed that easy forehand? If I hadn't blown that shot, I wouldn't be in this mess right now.*

And it's going to wander into the future: *If I miss another forehand, I will have let my team down.*

Instead, you must learn to focus on nothing but the task at hand. What do I want to accomplish here?

I want to hit a serve deep to the backhand and then look for a crosscourt volley or groundstroke.

That's a good start, but you can focus the task even more.

In order to hit a deep serve, I want to toss a bit more over my head and hit up and out.

Fear can't live in that moment. Fear does not exist in the present, only in the future. When you contain your thoughts to the task at hand—to the thing happening right now—you take the first step toward facing down pressure. (The philosophers of our day would argue that the situation is the same with the tiger: the threat is not what the tiger is doing now, but what it might do in the future. Deal with the tiger now: what do you need to do in order to neutralize the tiger in this moment? Not too many of us are sufficiently evolved with this thinking, so let's return to tennis where the mortal threat does not exist.)

The challenge of this way of thinking is that it could make you more mechanical. After all, we've spent no small amount of space talking about how the best performers turn their minds off altogether. Thinking about where to toss the ball and what swing plane to use hardly qualifies. It is still your ultimate goal to be able to perform on this match point in a free and mindless way and you can indeed get there from a focus on the task:

I want to hit this serve deep to the backhand, so I'm going to toss the ball a bit more over my head, not so much into the court. Then I'm going to look for an opportunity to hit crosscourt.

Okay, that's my task. I've got this. I can do this. I have each of those shots in my game. Now I just need to let myself do it. Let's just play.

That is healthy thinking. That puts you in a really good place to compete under pressure. If you combine that mental approach with some of the physical exercises discussed here, you come up with a working recipe for dealing with stress on the tennis court:

- Take one or two deep slow breaths.

- Make two or three long slow circles with your shoulder.

- Ask yourself what you want to get done on this next point.

- Identify the key fundamentals needed to accomplish that task.

- Recognize that those fundamentals are things you know how to do.

- Now turn your mind off and just let yourself do it.

I'm not here to suggest that any of this is easy. We all know the stakes we choose to associate with competitive tennis. The point I want to leave you with is that dealing with nerves and stress involves a set of skills that you can learn, practice, and master.

◆

One of my editors asked of this section: *Is there anything your partner can do to help?* Each of you has tasks in the moment that you can focus on, and while they might be different tasks, you can help one another identify them. It will be comforting to know that you both are in this moment.

Being True to Yourself...NOT

In what might be a record for the most times a book has referenced a particular chapter, we now arrive at the question whose answer might unlock the mysteries of human performance: what do you say to yourself or to your partner in the middle of a match to create a positive environment? In the last chapter, we laid out a blueprint for a healthy dialogue in stressful moments, and living in the moment like that would be a great way to play the entire match. But our minds aren't quite that perfect. They don't have on and off switches, and across two hours, countless thoughts, ideas, and whacked-out notions enter and exit our brains. What kind of coping mechanism exists for dealing with the mental flotsam of a tennis match?

To help answer that question, I will return to the 1980s and the week that I spent with Stefan Edberg while working on a profile of him for *Inside Tennis*. He led a group of five Swedish players in the world's Top 10, but he was very un-Swedelike, showcasing a one-handed backhand and an aggressive serve-and-volley style.

After a quarterfinal straight set victory over Brad Gilbert, he was asked about his almost-ridiculous 85% first serve proficiency, and according to my notes (which I still have...I know, I'm pathetic), here was his answer:

"When you get a high percentage of first serves in, it can be hard on your opponent. They don't get a rest."

One night later, Edberg defeated Paul Annacone to reach the final, but in that match, his first serve proficiency was barely 50%, about which he said the following: "Sometimes it's good to hit a lot of second serves, because your opponent expects to be able to do good things with them, and when they can't, that can be very frustrating." That is where things got interesting.

Me: You hit a lot of first serves yesterday and you said that you try to do that because it's tough on opponents.

Him: That was yesterday. Today is today. (Laughter in the press room)

Me: Are you saying that it was actually your strategy today to hit a lot of second serves?

Him: (Long pause) I'm saying that that's what worked for me today.

Me: That's funny, because it's the exact opposite of what you did yesterday.

Him: Is that bad?

Me: It seems as if you would want to be more consistent in your thinking.

Him: In tennis, you don't need to always be consistent. (More laughter)

This exchange resulted in no small amount of personal embarrassment in front of my peers, and people who were in the press room that day kidded me about it for years. "Hey Altman, have you given any good coaching advice to a pro lately?" "Has Edberg hired you as his sports psychologist yet?"

It was worth the ignominy, though, because that moment helped shape a guiding philosophy about competition:

It's okay to lie to yourself. In fact, it's a good thing.

Stefan Edberg didn't try to miss nearly half of his first serves against Annacone. That wasn't really his strategy. He was just spinning; he was choosing to look at the positive of an unexpected situation. *My first serve is way off today. That's okay, my second serve is strong, and maybe it will throw this guy off his rhythm.* Edberg was fooling himself and in so doing, he was choosing to adopt the most positive interpretation of the situation.

This plays out just about every day in one of the most innocent of ways: when you or someone else on the court frames a ball for a winner. "Hey, you paid for the entire racquet—you might as well use all of it."

Have you not heard that said at least a thousand times in your playing career? Did you intentionally hit the ball on the frame? Was that part of your strategy? Of course not—that's just what you say to stay positive. That's better than saying "That was the worst backhand in history, I don't deserve the point, and if the rules allowed it, I'd award it to you."

Even in doubles, tennis can be quite isolating. You face two people trying their hardest to break down your will, you are not allowed to have any coaching, and you need to find a way to figure it out. It's two against two, unless your attitude goes sour, then it becomes two and a half against two, as your critical half joins the other team. If instead, you make sure that your positive half is always on the court with you, then the half-person advantage could swing in your favor.

But it's not just attitude, however important that is to good performance. It's more than that. Harboring a belief in something can make it true. Showing faith in a concept can make it real. This isn't just mumbo-jumbo— it is a very real phenomenon that plays out in actual results. Let's review just a few of the references that I have made to this across the pages of this book.

Keep telling yourself that you are a better volleyer than she is. If you believe it, you can make it come true.

When I was younger, I believed that I could take any ball hit at me, no matter how hard, and volley it for a winner. This was an absurd notion, but I nonetheless parlayed it into a belief that nobody could beat me when I was in a good volleying position.

Proclaim that you can play equally well from the deuce and ad sides. Relish the opportunity to play from both sides. Soon, that enthusiasm will turn into confidence and that will compensate for whatever physical deficiency actually exists.

I said out loud so often that I love playing in the wind that other teams came to believe it themselves and sought to avoid me in windy conditions.

This topic always presents risks for a sports journalist who doesn't want to sound like a Pollyanna. *Think nice thoughts and say nice things and goodness will follow you.* There is also the risk to players that, in believing that anything is possible, they make stupid attempts at ridiculous shots. So a balance is needed here between what you do and how you respond to events.

And that is perhaps the key point: this is a reactive experience. When situations arise, when challenges present themselves, and when bad things happen, there is a range of responses available to you: anger, pouting, defiance, determination, and excitement. My golf buddies make merciless fun of me for putting a positive spin on bad play. *Your shot hit the cart path and bounced right into that water hazard. But you can drop on the other side of the water, where you would have a clear 220-yard shot at the green. And if you then sink that putt, hey it's a bogey!*

I proudly refer to myself as a pathological optimist and wear the kidding I get as a badge of honor. How can I take the worst possible situation and find something good in it? It's a good attitude to have at 5-5 in the third and it is a great exercise in problem-solving. Pessimists will not recognize possible alternate strategies because they are not looking for them. Optimists are always probing and the more you probe, the better you get at it. When optimists find a possible path forward, how do they know it will work? They don't, so they simply proclaim that it will. What's the harm?

How does this play out on the court? In countless ways...

- The sun has gone down and the lights haven't kicked in yet. Hmm, I wonder how that will impact our opponents. I'll bet they are going to have trouble with it. Let's take advantage!

- That wind is really swirling. We volley more than they do and if we can push volleys deep, the wind is going to wreak havoc on their passing shots. Let's do this!

- Her forehand is really strong. It's a good thing I know how to steer the ball to her backhand. That might really frustrate her.

- With a super-tiebreak as the third set and all of these quick points we're playing, this match is going to be over quickly. I love a good sprint...let's go!

- We are playing a full third set and we've already had six deuces. We're going to be out here for three hours. Excellent—I love a good marathon. We're going to just wear them down.

In some of these cases, the optimistic view uncovered legitimate strategies (volley more in the wind). And in some cases, they were completely contradictory—how can I love both sprints and marathons? As Edberg said, yesterday was yesterday and today is a new day. You do not have to be consistent in your beliefs; you are not arguing before the Grand Jury. You are seeking every opportunity to give your team a competitive advantage and if that means that you distort reality a bit, or depart from it entirely, then that's what you should do.

The problem is that, while I am a pathological optimist, I am not a pathological liar. I know that what I'm saying isn't true. I actually have pretty poor night vision and my optometrist will attest to it. In some cases, I'm not sure about a particular circumstance (are they really notorious chokers? Hmm, maybe) and reinforcing the belief is just what I need to embrace it. But in other cases, I really do know that I'm full of crap. That doesn't matter—I say it anyway. If it isn't completely true, I say it even louder. If I can't fool myself, I still might fool everyone else, including our opponents.

My favorite deception—for which, again, I am often made fun of—takes place when we have just secured a service break.

"Do you know what the score is?" I will ask my partner.

She either plays along or she takes the bait. "We're serving at 3-2."

"Nope, we're actually down a break, and now we have to fight like hell to get it back."

This is one of my favorite deceptions of all, as it guards against over-celebration of a service break. I also use it if we have escaped a 0-40 deficit and have reached the sanctuary of deuce, where it is tempting to relax. "It's 0-40 all over again, and we need to play one excellent point here."

I know this doesn't work for all players. I know there are players who would rather believe they are always ahead than always behind. They don't need to create the stress of deficit when it's not there; the real thing is bad enough. But for most of my partners and me, we love it. It keeps us hungry and focused.

One need look no further than the nearest political campaign for proof that vehemence can replace reality. Those television ads prey on the hope that if you say something long enough and loud enough, people will believe it. It will become a de-facto truth.

I would like to conclude by pointing out that I despise dishonest politicians and I do not advocate lying at work or to your loved ones. I reserve my advice about this bizarre behavior for times when you are locked in battle with opponents who seek to destroy you. So please don't sue me.

24

The True Meaning
Of Confidence

It might seem strange to wait until nearly the end to discuss what I identify in my introduction as one of the core tenets of this book. But it belongs here in my "mental" section and I consider it to be one of the most important concepts of all.

The word is pretty simple and nobody has to think too hard to grasp its meaning. You identify it as a good thing. You want to be confident. You want to play confidently. You want to exude confidence.

But do you actually know what it means? And more important, do you know how to harness it on demand when you are in a pressure situation and need it the most?

Many players do not. Let's say that you and your partner are up 6-1, 2-0, and you're cruising. Everything you hit goes in and you feel invincible. Backhand overheads that paint both lines…half-volley stabs…even your mishits are winners. You are hitting second serves almost as hard as firsts, and you have that wonderful feeling that you just can't miss. It's awesome. You love it. You're in the zone. It's a wonderful high.

But it's not confidence.

Don't misunderstand, playing out of your minds is a wonderful feeling and you and your partner hope it lasts all match. You should play quickly, in case the tennis gods have a timer, so you can get in as many points as you can while you are in this wonderful zone.

But this is not confidence, it's magic, and those two things are quite different. In fact, maybe they are opposites of one another. True confidence does not come from the feeling that you are invincible and can hit any shot imaginable. True confidence comes from knowing which shots you *really can hit*. Confidence is what you rely on once you leave the magic zone.

Here is a simple litmus test: That amazing backhand overhead that you hit deep into the corner of the court without a care in the world—would you attempt it at 6-6 in a tiebreaker? No? Why not? Because it is too risky, you say? Aren't you confident in your ability to hit it?

Well, no, you're not. Because you are a reasonably intelligent person and you know better. Being able to hit a shot while in the zone does not provide you with any confidence that you can also execute it when the pressure is on. In fact, it might make you feel unconfident about it, like you can only hit it when you are in an otherworldly state.

So what shots *can* you hit under pressure? Here are mine:

- Medium-pace serve to the backhand

- Crosscourt backhand volley

- Waist-high forehand volley

- Rolling forehand from an open stance

- Slice backhand

No matter what the situation, I harbor the belief that I can execute those five strokes. If I can orchestrate a point so that I would be attempting them, I would be quite confident in the outcome.

The time to attempt ridiculous shots is when you are in the zone and feel as if you can miss nothing. But when you find yourself in a must-make situation, you need to know what shots you really can hit.

When you find that out, you will be a truly confident tennis player.

Drills and Practice

I harbor deep resentment for book authors who preach to readers on how to practice and what to do with their time off the court. I reserve a special type of scorn for those who expect that a tennis player will take notes, fill out workbooks, and take them onto the court for structured practice sessions.

Give me a break.

We're all grownups here and you will decide for yourself how you will spend your free time and how you will spend your (often precious) court time. Your experience with this book will not be diminished by your not taking notes or by not designing elaborate practice sessions to work on specific concepts or techniques.

So in the most unpreachy way possible, here are a few thoughts on practicing.

Should You Really Practice How You Play?

If you were to conduct a poll, it is likely that four out of five teaching pros would recommend that tennis players approach practice matches the same way that they do league matches. The pros would speak to the value of getting used to the intensity of a real match, regulating energy levels, and focusing on crucial points. *Practice like you play,* as the grammatically-suspect expression goes.

This sounds like such good advice, why would only four out of five pros recommend it? It's kind of like the chewing gum commercial—would you like to have as your dentist the one out of five who does *not* recommend sugarless gum to patients who chew gum?

Yes, this is great advice…until it isn't. If you are one of the few unable to practice the way you play, you begin to wonder if you are defective. Take it from me, you're not—the conventional advice simply does not apply to you.

Indeed, not everyone benefits from practicing tennis at 100% intensity. I'm one of those people, so I know the frustration of trying in vain to conform. I also know that I have caused frustration among folks I play practice matches with who play them earnestly when I don't.

It is nearly impossible for me to play as well or as hard in practice as I might in a match. I am not able to focus as intently, I can't fool myself into believing that it matters, and I am constantly wanting to experiment with stuff. "What side would you like to play," my partner might ask me before a practice match, to which my response might very well be, "Well, I played the ad side last night, so just for variety, I'd choose the deuce side." How's that for brilliant strategy?

I estimate that I lose close to 75% of the practice sets I play. The year that I went undefeated in the 5.5s, I lost almost every one of my practice matches. This was a source of angst for me at one point, as if there was something wrong with me.

And then I made peace with it. I concluded that it was perfectly fine to suck in practice as long as I played well in competition, and for me that is part of the dynamic: It is vital for me to distinguish between matches that matter and matches that don't. I don't want to bring sameness to the experiences; I want them to feel different. I thrive on the belief that matches are unique and special. They are not just like practice for me and it doesn't serve me well to act or pretend otherwise.

I don't intentionally try to lose practice matches. It's not like I try to play badly in practice. Well, that's not entirely true—sometimes I will intentionally put myself in holes just to see if I can climb out of them. I might play to an opponent's strengths instead of away from them, akin to playing basketball with ankle weights or swinging a baseball bat with a donut. I just find it impossible to play with intensity or focus in practice, and that usually translates to a visible dropoff in my level of play.

This is normally harmless, unless you are joining a new team where a captain is forming a first impression of you from a Tuesday night practice session. Or worse, you are asked to play a challenge match—talk about the bane of my existence! I have never learned how to treat challenge matches like league matches and have had a few epic fails while playing them.

Once a friend and teammate named Leigh recruited me onto a team and then had to bail me out when he and the captain were watching me do my usual thing in practice: Serving intentionally into big forehands, attempting half-volley lobs, climbing out of 0-40 holes and then losing deuce points on purpose just to try to do it again, and generally playing as if I couldn't give a crap about the results.

"I thought you said this guy was good?" the captain reportedly asked of Leigh. "Um, he does better in matches," he replied, hoping that he had not stuck his neck out too far. When I left the court, Leigh intercepted me. "Next time, don't suck so bad—you make *me* look bad." Then he laughed, shoved a beer in my hand, and clanked it with his own.

Why am I telling you all this? I'm not trying to convert you to this way of thinking, as if it is a superior way to practice. It's not, otherwise four out of five pros would advocate for it. But if you already think that way—if you are wired that way, as I am—don't fight it. Accept it as an integral part of the way you compete, turn it into a positive, and wear it proudly.

Your teammates will deal with it, especially if you bring your A game to matches. And if you ever find out how to play well in challenge matches, email me and tell me your secret!

I Hate All Drills...Except for These Two

I'm bad at drills. I lack the temperament, just like I can't swim laps or go running. The specter of hitting 50 forehands crosscourt, then down the line, then backhands crosscourt, etc., and then doing it again two days later—that would be enough to compel me to give up the game. And I am not even sure if those kinds of drills would be any good for my doubles game.

But there are two volley drills that I could participate in all day. They are fun, excellent for doubles players, and very good exercise. I recommend them for all doubles players, irrespective of gender, aptitude, or temperament.

Brute force bashoff

Two players or two teams face one another from their respective service lines and one side puts the ball in play. Your objective is simple: to work your way to a place where you can hit down on a volley. You are not allowed to hit the ball away from your opponent, nor can you lob. The only way to win a point is to hit right through the other person.

In this drill, the lines between offense and defense are quite subtle, because the rules forbid you from practicing true defense. All you can do is volley back and hope that you can keep your opponent(s) at bay. If you can reach the ball early enough to be able to hit down by even just a degree or two, you create a tiny advantage that you can then cultivate. And you do that by closing and trying to force your opponent to hit up. And when he or she does, you lower the boom.

Lots of body parts are at risk in this drill, which is further incentive to try to seize the offensive early. If you want to keep score, fine—normally, I just play that when you lose the point, you have to put the next ball in play, and you must start the point with an underhand serve.

This is excellent for developing quickness, for ball-tracking, and for closing on the net and finishing points assertively.

Feather contest

Next comes another front-court drill that is nearly the complete opposite: a duel in which you are never allowed to hit down on the ball. The only other rule is that if a ball bounces beyond the service line, it is out. This drill becomes extremely aerobic, as strategy translates to seizing upon angles and stretching shots and coverage across the width of the court. You are forever anticipating and trying to read how the ball might come off of your opponent's racquet. If you can get to the ball quickly, you create extreme angles to exploit, which in turn exposes you to angles. There is a lot of cat-and-mouse as you jockey for position, trying to recognize when to play a ball on the bounce and when to move in and take control of a point. And because you can't hit down on any ball, winning a point usually involves an orchestration of several shots.

You'll be breathing hard after just a few minutes and your legs will be dead soon after. It is a terrific workout and exercise to cultivate anticipation and quick reaction. This drill easily accommodates a partner, so doubles teams can go at it and various king-of-the-hill contests can be arranged between larger groups.

As to the rumors and allegations that my friends and I have participated in this drill while holding beers in our off-hand, well, I simply have no comment about that.

The Often-Painful Notion of "All In"

T his chapter probably belongs in the Going Mental section; instead, I am choosing to conclude all of my thoughts with it and am suspending conventional numbering for it. It attempts to bring to light one of the most elusive and timeless concepts of all: how to truly perform at your best in the most vulnerable way.

That is an unusual word to use—what does it mean to be vulnerable? Being vulnerable is bad, right? As in, "you are vulnerable to the lob" or "his second serve made him vulnerable." In this context, it has a different meaning and it is one of the best qualities you can exhibit while competing.

Excuses, excuses

Perhaps the best way to frame this topic is to identify some typical post-match analyses:

I would have played better if I hadn't hurt my hamstring last week. I couldn't quite give it my all out there.

When the wind picked up, it played havoc with my contact lenses. I did my best after that, but I just couldn't see well enough to play aggressively.

My new partner and I don't quite gel. Perhaps I would do better with someone else.

We were winning in the second set when there was that commotion in the park. That really threw off my game.

3.5, my butt! That guy was at least a 4.0; what a sandbagger! No wonder we lost—I'm going to lodge a formal protest.

When the _____ happened, it caused me to _____, and that kept me from _____ing.

What do all of these statements have in common? If you said that they all occurred following a defeat, that is not necessarily the case. Here are a bunch of common pre-match excuses:

I just need to tell you, my shoulder has been really hurting lately. I'm going to do my best, though.

I have this massive deadline at work, so if I'm a bit distracted today, that's why.

I've had a cold all week, and while I feel better today, I'm not sure how much energy I will have.

This _____ happened, which is preventing me from _____ing, and that is the reason that I might not _____ today.

In each of these scenarios, there are forces being identified that prevented or might prevent the person from playing to potential. Each one of these statements points to an outside agency that has exerted some influence on the player.

These all seem like typical statements made by aging amateurs, and as such, appear on their face to be innocuous. After all, who among us hasn't experienced a _____ that has kept us from _____ing? They are just excuses, right? We all make them—we're not professionals, we're no longer 22 years old, we can't focus as we used to, and when things bother us, that hurts our game. Stop the presses, right?

The problem with an excuse is that it becomes like a narcotic: it feels really comforting, and before you know it, you become dependent upon having one. Having an excuse makes it easier to deal with a loss, and if you should somehow win instead, you become positively heroic! "Wow, did you see Jane out there with a sprained ankle? She almost pulled out that match—what a trooper she is!" With positive strokes like that, Jane is going to want to sprain her ankle before every match.

Excuses are defense mechanisms: they protect us from the pain and trauma of a loss. *Yes, I lost that match, but it was because of my sprained ankle. If I were 100%, it would have been different.* You see how protected your ego is thanks to that sprained ankle? *He didn't really beat me legitimately because I wasn't playing at 100%.*

Again, these seem like innocent enough statements but they are actually quite insidious. Ego shielding is extremely habit-forming—when you continue to find reasons why you are unable to compete at 100%, you increase the likelihood that you will *never* compete at 100%.

Because what happens if you are at 100%? What if you have no impediments to performing at your best? What if you leave it all out there? And you still do not win? What does that say about you? It says that you were not good enough. You were beaten. Your opponents are better than you.

You are a loser.

How does that feel? That hurts way more than the sprained ankle, doesn't it?

Learning how to lose

"To learn to succeed, you must first learn to fail."

Before I reveal the author of this quote, who also authored the following ones in this section, we need to dissect it. In order to learn how to win, you need to learn how to put yourself in a position where total failure is a distinct possibility. Not partial failure—not having lost a match because some condition prevented you from playing your best. You must experience total failure—losing when you were completely prepared to play your best.

And when that happens, you must learn to face it down and accept it. Perhaps you already know how! to do that; some players accept defeat more easily than others. Irrespective, you must reach a point where you can accept that you played your heart out and still lost.

*"I can accept failure, everyone fails at
something. But I can't accept not trying."*

When you shield your ego and create conditions where excuses exist, it is impossible to put forth maximum effort. Your conscious mind is too busy managing your excuse and that gets in the way of performance.

I know exactly how that feels because I've done it. I remember having a nagging knee injury and yet agreeing to play a match. I should have subscribed to Rafael Nadal's credo: "If you set foot on the court, it means that you are 100% ready to play. No excuses." I should have declined. Or I should have just kept my mouth shut. Instead, I announced to all of my teammates that I might not be moving as well as usual. Once I said it, I could feel a certain anxiety dissipating, as if the stakes had dropped. Good thing, too: we drew a team that hadn't lost yet that season. How could we possibly expect to compete when I was hampered? There would be no shame or trauma in losing this match.

We were down an early break and I was comfortable just trying to make a respectable showing, which I figured 6-3 set scores would accomplish. But then we broke back to even the set and had break points at 3-4 and at 4-5 (the second one being a set point). I managed my injury better than expected and suddenly, we were totally in that first set. But when we failed to convert either of those break points, and then lost our own serve at 5-5, my injury mysteriously got worse. I was in some strange phantom zone where I couldn't figure out where to best spend my emotional energy—trying to win a tennis match or servicing my injury. I must have experienced over a dozen mini dramas with each game won and lost. *C'mon, Rick, you can do this…they held serve, well, what did you expect, you can't move…set point for us, wow, how'd that happen…now they're serving for the set, well, you were respectable.*

*"You must expect great things of
yourself before you can do them."*

I was in the wrong frame of mind to compete, and while the injury might have triggered this attitude shift, the attitude itself became a larger impediment than the injury. My frame of mind set the expectation level for the match, and it was way off. Set aside that the tennis gods invented ibuprofen just for this situation. And also set aside the phenomenon that sometimes you can actually play better with a minor injury, as you stay more within yourself and often play more intelligently. Forget all of that—I had already convinced myself that peak performance would not be possible on this day, and that was too high of a hurdle to cross.

You have probably attended a presentation of some sort where the first thing the speaker said was, "You'll have to bear with me, I was just given this assignment yesterday." That person is hoping to lower the stakes by setting your expectation level. But in so doing, the speaker is also lowering his or her own expectation level, and that is never a good thing. *Never!*

Playing the excuse game messes with the expectations that you should set for yourself. The only way that you can expect great things is if you know that you are doing everything possible to perform at your best.

"What is love? Love is playing every game as if it's your last."

This quote, from arguably the best player in the history of his sport, reminds me of that wonderful ballad from John McGraw about his father being diagnosed with cancer. He learned to "Live Like You Were Dying," and experience every moment as if it were his last.

If you knew that today's match would be the last one you would ever play, would you let an injury get in your way? Would you allow any potential excuse to affect your attitude? No, you'd go for it—it's your last tennis match ever! You'd go sky diving, Rocky Mountain climbing, you'd go 2.7 seconds on that bull, and you would play the best tennis match of your life.

"I've missed more than 9000 shots in my career. I've lost almost 300 games. And 26 times, I've been trusted to take the game winning shot and missed. I've failed over and over and over again in my life. And that is why I succeed."

Michael Jordan won five consecutive NBA championships because he was able to first make peace with losing. He learned to define success, not by wins and losses, but by effort, expectation, and attitude.

Learning to be "all in"

Once you stop measuring your self-esteem by wins and losses, you take the first step toward peak performance, and that brings us back to the concept of vulnerability. In my profession, I teach company leaders to face a group of people—maybe friendly, maybe not—and show their most genuine self. If they are going to truly engage an audience, they can't make excuses, hide behind bad PowerPoint slides, or even stand behind a lectern. They must face their audience, tell their story, and accept whatever fate comes their way. I refer to it as "being naked" in front of the audience, and it is about as vulnerable as one might ever feel.

Same thing for the Broadway performer. She might be playing a role, but what she is really doing is exposing her soul to her audience, knowing that the next morning the *New York Times* might love her or hate her. It is that vulnerability that allows her to give the best possible performance.

Can you do that on the tennis court? Can you adopt the attitude that there will never again be any excuses or reasons for not putting forth your very best effort? Can you vow that you will always do everything within your power to perform at your best? That you will spill your guts and your heart on the court and then accept whatever result follows?

If you can go "all in" like this, you will begin to measure your self-worth differently. Losing will no longer feel like the worst thing that could happen to you; failing to make the right kind of effort will feel worse.

Those two imposters

If you go back and review this chapter, you will see that I mention winning infrequently, and the word "victory" does not appear even once. For the best competitors in our sport, winning is not the primary goal. They are not "trying" to win; they are placing themselves in the best possible position to perform to potential. Winning becomes the by-product of that.

Most tennis enthusiasts have read the famous excerpt from the 1910 Rudyard Kipling poem "If." Here is a bit more from the four-stanza work:

If you can dream—and not make dreams your master;
If you can think—and not make thoughts your aim;
If you can meet with triumph and disaster
And treat those two impostors just the same;

If you can make one heap of all your winnings
And risk it on one turn of pitch-and-toss,
And lose, and start again at your beginnings
And never breathe a word about your loss;

Yours is the Earth and everything that's in it,
And—which is more—you'll be a Man my son!

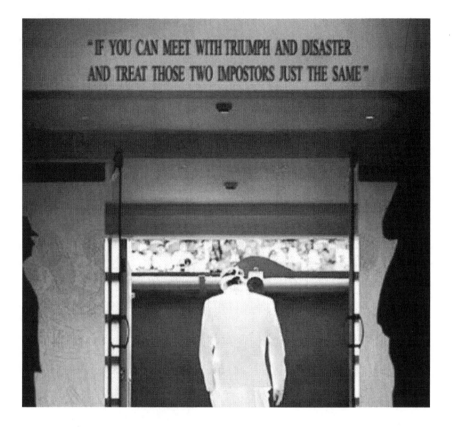

Why did the officials at the All England Club choose to inscribe these two lines above the entry to Centre Court? It helps remind the very best tennis players in the world that winning is not the aim and losing is not to be feared. Their quest is to take to the arena, with the eyes of the world upon them, and summon their inner strength, passion, and love in order to dedicate themselves to the quest for peak performance. If they are able to do that, they can accept any outcome.

♦

If it works for the players at Wimbledon, perhaps it will also work for you and me.

www.KillerDoubles.net

Index

Does a book on doubles need an index? We think not, but if you disagree, please let us know at ricka@killerdoubles.net.

68377660R00092

Made in the USA
Lexington, KY
09 October 2017